MICROSOFT COPIL(USER GUIDE 2025

The Essential Companion to Navigating the Future of AI-Powered Productivity to Harness the Full Potential of This Intelligent Tool

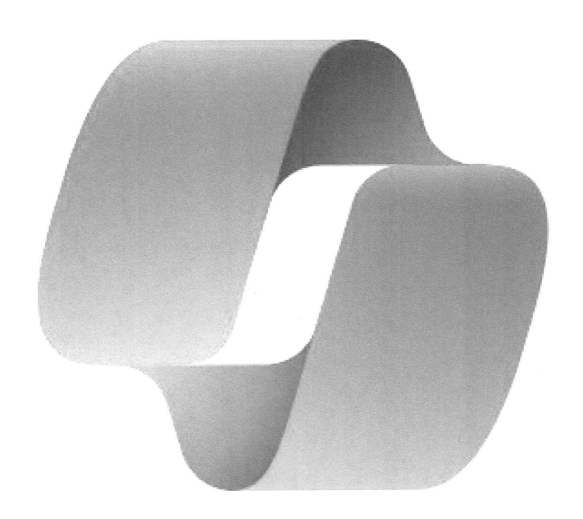

MANUEL W. SUNDBERG

TABLE OF CONTENTS

DISCLAIMER

The contents of this book are provided for informational and entertainment purposes only. The author and publisher do not make any representations or warranties regarding the accuracy, applicability, completeness, or suitability of the contents for any purpose.

The information in this book is based on the author's personal experiences, research, and opinions, and should not be considered a substitute for professional advice. Readers are advised to consult appropriate professionals regarding their specific situations.

The author and publisher are not liable for any loss, injury, or damage allegedly arising from the information or suggestions in this book. Any reliance on such information is at the reader's own risk.

The inclusion of third-party resources, websites, or references does not imply endorsement or responsibility for their content or services.

Readers are encouraged to use their own discretion and judgment when applying the information or recommendations in this book to their own lives.

Thank you for reading and understanding this disclaimer

CHAPTER ONE
INTRODUCTION TO MICROSOFT COPILOT 2025

Microsoft Copilot 2025 is the latest iteration of Microsoft's AI-powered assistant, designed to enhance productivity, streamline workflows, and provide intelligent assistance across various applications and services. Built on advanced AI models, Copilot integrates seamlessly with Microsoft 365, Windows, and other platforms, offering users a smarter and more efficient way to work.

With the increasing demand for AI-driven solutions, Microsoft Copilot 2025 leverages natural language processing (NLP) and machine learning to provide contextual insights, automate repetitive tasks, and facilitate collaboration. This powerful tool is engineered to adapt to user preferences, offering personalized suggestions and real-time support across different work environments.

Key Features of Microsoft Copilot 2025

1. **Enhanced AI Capabilities** – Utilizes the latest advancements in generative AI to provide more accurate and context-aware responses.

2. **Deep Integration with Microsoft 365** – Works seamlessly within Word, Excel, PowerPoint, Outlook, and Teams to enhance productivity.

3. **Advanced Natural Language Understanding** – Interprets complex queries and delivers precise results, making it easier for users to interact with software intuitively.

4. **Task Automation and Efficiency** – Reduces manual effort by automating repetitive processes such as summarizing emails, generating reports, and scheduling meetings.

5. **Security and Compliance** – Incorporates Microsoft's enterprise-grade security measures to ensure data protection and compliance with industry standards.

6. **Customization and Personalization** – Adapts to user behavior and preferences, providing tailored recommendations and workflow optimizations.

7. **Collaboration and Communication Support** – Assists with drafting emails, summarizing meetings, and generating insights to improve team collaboration.

Applications and Benefits

- **For Businesses:** Enhances operational efficiency by automating administrative tasks and improving decision-making with AI-driven insights.

- **For Educators & Students:** Assists with research, document creation, and knowledge retention, making learning more interactive.

- **For Developers:** Provides AI-powered coding suggestions and debugging assistance to speed up software development.

- **For Everyday Users:** Simplifies digital interactions, from composing messages to managing personal tasks efficiently.

Microsoft Copilot 2025 is a transformative AI assistant that redefines how users interact with digital tools, offering smarter solutions for work and productivity. As AI continues to evolve, Copilot stands as a testament to Microsoft's commitment to innovation, making AI more accessible and beneficial for everyone.

<u>Target Audience</u>

The **target audience** for **Microsoft Copilot in 2025** can be broadly categorized based on industry, professional roles, and use cases. Here's a breakdown:

1. Business & Enterprise Users

- **Executives & Managers** – For strategic decision-making, reports, and productivity enhancement.

- **Knowledge Workers** – Professionals like analysts, consultants, and marketers who use Copilot for content creation, research, and automation.

- **IT & Developers** – Those integrating Copilot into workflows, coding, and managing enterprise AI solutions.

- **Customer Service Teams** – Using AI-powered assistance for responding to inquiries and managing customer relationships.

2. Education & Research

- **Students & Educators** – For learning support, academic writing, research assistance, and curriculum development.

- **Researchers** – For summarizing literature, generating insights, and automating data analysis.

3. Creatives & Content Professionals

- **Writers & Journalists** – Using Copilot for drafting articles, editing, and summarizing content.

- **Graphic Designers & Video Editors** – Leveraging AI-powered design assistance in tools like Microsoft Designer and Clipchamp.

4. Healthcare & Medical Professionals

- **Doctors & Nurses** – For clinical documentation, patient record summaries, and medical research.

- **Healthcare Administrators** – Using AI for appointment scheduling, data management, and efficiency improvements.

5. Small Business Owners & Entrepreneurs

- **Startups & SMBs** – Using Copilot for business planning, customer engagement, and financial management.

- **Freelancers & Consultants** – Leveraging AI for proposal writing, social media management, and automation.

6. Government & Legal Professionals

- **Legal Experts** – For contract drafting, legal research, and document summarization.

- **Government Officials** – Enhancing policy analysis, report writing, and citizen communication.

7. Everyday Consumers

- **General Users** – Utilizing Copilot in Microsoft 365 for emails, scheduling, personal organization, and productivity.

- **Gamers & Tech Enthusiasts** – Leveraging AI for gaming insights, strategies, and automation in Xbox or Windows.

CHAPTER TWO
GETTING STARTED WITH MICROSOFT COPILOT 2025

Prerequisites and System Requirements

To effectively use Microsoft Copilot in 2025, users need to meet the following **prerequisites** and **system requirements**:

Prerequisites

Microsoft 365 Subscription (For Enterprise & Personal Use)

- Copilot is integrated into Microsoft 365 apps (Word, Excel, PowerPoint, Outlook, Teams, etc.).

- Requires a valid **Microsoft 365 Business, Enterprise, or Personal** plan.

Copilot Pro or Business Plan (For Advanced Features)

- Some advanced AI features are available in **Copilot Pro** (for individuals) or **Copilot for Microsoft 365** (for businesses).

Microsoft Account & Azure AD (For Enterprise Users)

- Business users must have an **Azure Active Directory (AAD)** account for enterprise security and access management.

Internet Connection

- A stable **high-speed internet connection** is required for real-time AI processing and cloud-based features.

Cloud Integration (For Business Users)

- Enterprises should ensure compatibility with **Microsoft Azure, OneDrive, and SharePoint** for cloud-based collaboration.

Windows 11 or Latest Updates on Windows 10

- Copilot is deeply integrated into **Windows 11** and **Windows 10 (latest updates required)**.

System Requirements
For Windows Devices

Operating System:

- **Windows 11 (Preferred)** or **Windows 10 (with latest updates)**

Processor (CPU):

- **Intel Core i5 (10th Gen or later) / AMD Ryzen 5 (or equivalent) / Apple M1+ (Mac via web app)**

- AI-optimized processors (e.g., Intel Core Ultra, Qualcomm Snapdragon X Elite) recommended for better performance.

Memory (RAM):

- **Minimum: 8GB RAM**

- **Recommended: 16GB RAM** (for AI-intensive tasks like data analysis, design, and automation)

Storage:

- **Minimum: 256GB SSD**

- **Recommended: 512GB SSD or higher**

Graphics (GPU):

- Integrated **Intel UHD/ Iris Xe / AMD Radeon** (for basic use)

- **Dedicated NVIDIA RTX / AMD Radeon RX** (for AI-powered creative tools)

Display:

- **Full HD (1080p) or higher resolution** for optimal UI experience

For Mobile & Web Users

iOS & Android:

- Requires the **latest version of Microsoft 365 apps**

- Recommended **iOS 16+** (iPhone) or **Android 12+**

Web Browsers (For Copilot Web Access):

- **Microsoft Edge (Recommended)**

- **Google Chrome, Safari, or Firefox (Latest versions)**

Additional Considerations

AI-Optimized Hardware (For Enhanced Performance)

- Devices with **NPU (Neural Processing Unit)** support will experience **faster AI processing**.

- Examples: **Surface Pro 10, Copilot+ PCs, Qualcomm Snapdragon AI Laptops**

Enterprise Security & Compliance

- Organizations may require **Microsoft Entra ID (formerly Azure AD)** for identity management.

- Compliance with **GDPR, HIPAA, and ISO 27001** for data security.

Copilot in Microsoft Teams & Outlook

- Businesses should enable **Teams AI plugins** for real-time assistance in meetings and emails.

Installation and Setup

To install and set up Microsoft Copilot in 2025, follow these steps. Note that Microsoft Copilot may be integrated into Microsoft 365 apps like Word, Excel, Outlook, etc., or offered as part of a broader productivity suite. The installation and setup process could vary depending on the specific Microsoft product you're using.

1. Ensure Eligibility and Subscription

- Microsoft Copilot is available for specific Microsoft 365 plans. Ensure that you have the correct subscription, such as Microsoft 365 Enterprise or Microsoft 365 Business Standard.

- Check if the Copilot feature is included in your plan by reviewing the available features on the Microsoft website.

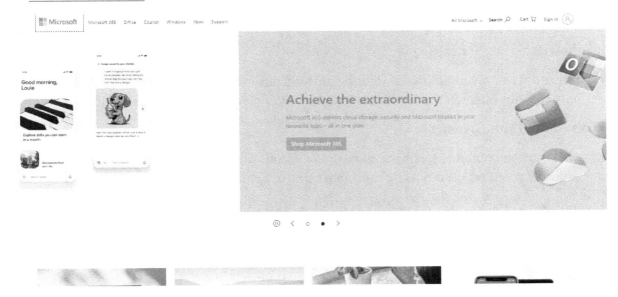

2. Update Microsoft 365 Applications

- Make sure your Microsoft 365 apps (Word, Excel, PowerPoint, Outlook, etc.) are up to date. You can do this by:
  - Open any Microsoft app (e.g., Word).
  - Go to **File** > **Account** > **Update Options** > **Update Now**.

3. Access Copilot Features

- Once your subscription is eligible and apps are updated, the Copilot feature should automatically be integrated into the apps you use.

- In apps like Word or Excel, look for a **Copilot** or **AI-powered assistant** section within the tools or in the ribbon toolbar.

- You can activate Copilot by clicking on the available Copilot button or typing commands in the search bar or prompt box, depending on the app.

4. Set Up Permissions

- Microsoft Copilot may require administrative permissions or Microsoft Azure Active Directory configurations for enterprise environments.

- IT administrators should review the permissions and security settings to ensure that the AI features are accessible and comply with company policies.

5. Start Using Copilot

- In apps like Word, Excel, or Outlook, Copilot will offer suggestions, generate content, automate tasks, and assist with data analysis or writing.

- To begin, you can start typing your request (e.g., "Write a summary of this document" or "Generate a report on sales data from this sheet") and Copilot will assist.

- Use natural language for instructions, and Copilot will provide relevant outputs based on your command.

6. Customize Copilot Settings

- Depending on the app, there might be customization options in settings where you can adjust how Copilot interacts with you, such as tone or content generation preferences.

7. Feedback and Improvements

- Microsoft encourages feedback to improve Copilot's features. You may be able to share your experiences or report any issues through built-in feedback mechanisms within the apps.

For the most up-to-date instructions, it's a good idea to consult Microsoft's official support page or the Microsoft 365 admin centre if you're managing the deployment for an organization.

First-Time Configuration

To set up Microsoft Copilot for the first time in 2025, follow these steps to ensure proper configuration, whether you're using it on a personal or business account:

1. Ensure Prerequisites

- **Microsoft 365 Subscription**: Make sure you're subscribed to a plan that includes Microsoft Copilot. It is typically available for Microsoft 365 Enterprise and Business subscriptions.

- **Microsoft Account**: Ensure that you have a valid Microsoft account, and that it is linked to your subscription.

- **Admin Access** (for businesses): If you're an administrator in a business setting, ensure that you have the necessary permissions to activate Copilot for your team.

2. Install/Update Microsoft 365 Apps
Microsoft Copilot is integrated into apps like Word, Excel, Outlook, and Teams.

- Ensure that your Microsoft 365 apps are up to date to gain access to Copilot. Follow these steps:
  - Open a Microsoft 365 app (e.g., Word).
  - Go to **File** > **Account** > **Update Options** > **Update Now**.

3. Activate Copilot in Your Microsoft 365 Account

- **For Individual Users**:
  - Once your subscription is activated and apps are updated, Copilot should automatically be enabled for your Microsoft 365 apps. You may not need to take additional action beyond signing in.

- **For Admins (Business Accounts)**:
  - **Admin Center**: Access the Microsoft 365 Admin Center.
  - Go to **Settings** > **Services & add-ins**.
  - Look for the **Copilot settings** and ensure that Copilot is enabled across the relevant apps.
  - You may need to configure user permissions and enable specific features to allow employees to use Copilot.

4. Configure Copilot Settings (Personal and Business Use)

- Once Copilot is activated, you may be able to customize its behavior.
  - **For Individual Users**: Some apps might allow you to adjust Copilot preferences, such as the level of detail or tone for content generation.
  - **For Businesses**: If you're an admin, review and configure the Copilot settings to match your organization's needs. You can enable or restrict access for certain users or apps and define how Copilot integrates with workflows.

5. Set Permissions (For Admins)

- If you're an IT admin, ensure that the proper roles and permissions are set for users in your organization.
- Go to the **Microsoft 365 Admin Center** > **Roles** > **Assign Copilot Permissions** to specific user groups.

6. First-Time Use

- Once Copilot is enabled, launch the Microsoft 365 app where you wish to use Copilot (Word, Excel, Outlook, etc.).
- In apps like Word or Excel, you'll find Copilot either as an integrated feature or in a new section of the toolbar.
  - For example, in Word, you might see a **Copilot** icon in the **Home** tab or on the right side of the screen.

o Start by typing a command, such as "Summarize this document" or "Create a financial analysis from this data," and Copilot will generate the output.

7. Training Copilot (Optional)

- Some users may need to train Copilot to better understand specific commands or preferences. This can typically be done through user interaction by giving feedback or by using Copilot consistently for various tasks.

8. Security and Privacy Settings

- Review and configure security settings to ensure that Copilot operates within your organization's security standards.
    - o **Data Handling**: Make sure that the way Copilot interacts with your data complies with your organization's privacy policies.
    - o **Compliance Settings**: For business accounts, ensure that Copilot follows legal, compliance, and regulatory requirements regarding data processing.

9. Provide Feedback

- After your first use, Microsoft encourages users to provide feedback to help refine Copilot's features.
- Use the feedback options in your Microsoft 365 app or admin portal to report issues or suggest improvements.

10. Monitor Usage (For Admins)

- For businesses, monitor how users are interacting with Copilot to ensure it's being used effectively.
- Track Copilot-related activities and user satisfaction using the Microsoft 365 Admin Center.

By following these steps, you'll have Microsoft Copilot properly set up and configured for optimal use, whether you're an individual or an admin managing a business account.

Basic Navigation and User Interface

Microsoft Copilot integrates directly into Microsoft 365 applications like Word, Excel, PowerPoint, and Outlook, offering a streamlined user interface designed to help you navigate and interact with the tool efficiently. Here's a guide to basic navigation and the user interface for Copilot:

1. Accessing Copilot

- **Microsoft Word**:
  - Once Copilot is activated, you'll likely see a **Copilot** icon in the toolbar. This could appear as a **lightbulb** or **AI icon** depending on the app version.
  - Alternatively, you might find a **Copilot** option in the **Home** or **Insert** tabs, depending on the app and task.

- **Microsoft Excel**:
  - In Excel, look for Copilot in the **Data** or **Formulas** tabs. You may also see it in the **Home** tab or as a floating pane on the side.

- **Microsoft Outlook**:
  - Copilot can assist you with email composition or data insights. You might find it in the email composition window or as a sidebar option.

2. Basic Navigation and User Interface in Each App

Microsoft Word

- **Copilot Integration**: Copilot in Word helps with writing, summarizing, formatting, and generating content. You can interact with Copilot by:
  - Clicking on the **Copilot** button in the toolbar.
  - Using the search bar or command box to type specific requests (e.g., "Summarize this document").

- **Sidebar/Panel**: A Copilot panel might appear on the right side of the screen, where you can provide instructions, and Copilot will generate content or suggestions.

- **Prompts**: You can type prompts such as "Create a meeting agenda," and Copilot will help you with the structure and content.

Microsoft Excel

- **Copilot Integration**: In Excel, Copilot assists with data analysis, summarizing large datasets, and creating charts. Copilot can help generate formulas or visualize data.

  - You can click on the **Copilot** button in the ribbon, usually in the **Data** tab.

  - Copilot might open in a **side panel** where it guides you through various tasks, such as summarizing trends or creating pivot tables.

- **Interactive Data Analysis**: You can type commands such as "Create a trend chart from this data" or "Generate a summary of this table," and Copilot will perform the task.

Microsoft PowerPoint

- **Copilot Integration**: In PowerPoint, Copilot can help generate slides, create presentations from outlines, or suggest designs and content.

  - Copilot will likely be accessible in the **Home** or **Design** tab as a button or command.

  - A **sidebar** may appear where Copilot can generate text, suggest design ideas, or organize content into slides.

- **Slide Generation**: You can input prompts like "Create a presentation on climate change," and Copilot will automatically generate slides based on your input.

Microsoft Outlook

- **Copilot Integration**: In Outlook, Copilot helps with drafting emails, summarizing threads, and suggesting responses.

  - You'll see a **Copilot** button in the email composition window or a **suggestions panel**.

  - Copilot might also assist with scheduling meetings or managing email threads more efficiently.

- **Email Composition**: For instance, you can prompt Copilot by saying, "Write a follow-up email to this client," and it will draft the message for you.

3. Core Features and Functions

Search and Command Box

- In most apps, you'll see a search or command box where you can type natural language commands to ask Copilot for help (e.g., "Generate a report" or "Summarize this email thread").

- This is an essential feature for quick access to Copilot's capabilities.

Sidebar or Panel

- Many Microsoft 365 apps integrate Copilot through a floating **sidebar** or **side panel** on the right-hand side of your screen.

- This panel typically displays the tasks Copilot can assist with and allows you to refine requests or view generated content.

Toolbar or Ribbon Integration

- Copilot might be integrated directly into the main toolbar or ribbon of the app. It could appear as a dedicated button or icon like **Copilot**, **AI Assistant**, or **Power Assistant**.

Contextual Suggestions

- Copilot is designed to provide **contextual suggestions** based on the content you're working with. For example:

    o In Word, it can offer writing suggestions, summaries, or formatting options.

    o In Excel, it can recommend data visualizations or suggest formulas.

4. Basic Commands and Interactions

- **Natural Language Inputs**: Type requests in natural language, such as:

    o "Summarize the meeting notes."

    o "Analyse this data and find trends."

    o "Create a presentation based on these bullet points."

- **Copilot Suggestions**: Based on your content, Copilot will make relevant suggestions. For example, in Word, it might suggest adding a heading or in Excel, it might recommend creating a pivot table from the data.

5. Navigating Copilot's Outputs

- Once Copilot generates content or suggestions, you can:

    o **Edit the output** directly within the app.

    o **Accept or reject** the suggestions provided by Copilot.

    o **Refine or ask for more details** by clicking on the generated content and typing further requests.

6. Customizing the Experience

- **For Personal Use**: You may be able to personalize Copilot's responses (e.g., preferred tone, level of detail).

- **For Businesses**: Admins can customize Copilot's interactions, permissions, and available features to suit organizational needs. This might include restricting access to specific Copilot features or apps.

By familiarizing yourself with these basic navigation elements and user interface features, you'll be able to make the most out of Microsoft Copilot's integration into your Microsoft 365 suite.

CHAPTER THREE
FEATURES OF MICROSOFT COPILOT

Real-time Assistance and Suggestions

Microsoft Copilot offers real-time assistance and suggestions to improve productivity, enhance workflows, and provide valuable insights as you work within Microsoft 365 apps like Word, Excel, PowerPoint, Outlook, and more. Here's how to make the most of this feature:

1. How Real-Time Assistance Works

- **Context-Aware Help**: Copilot provides real-time suggestions based on the content you're working on. It understands the context of your document, data, or email and makes recommendations accordingly. For example, if you're writing an email in Outlook, Copilot can suggest responses, summarize email threads, or even create replies for you.

- **Automatic Adaptation**: As you continue working, Copilot adapts and refines its suggestions. It's designed to understand what you're doing in real time and offer appropriate help without interrupting your workflow.

2. Real-Time Assistance in Key Microsoft 365 Apps

Microsoft Word

- **Writing Assistance**: While typing in a document, Copilot will offer suggestions on improving sentence structure, grammar, and style. For instance, if you write a long paragraph, Copilot might suggest breaking it down into smaller, clearer sections or provide alternative wording.

- **Content Generation**: Copilot can help generate content in real time based on prompts like "Create an outline for this document" or "Write a summary of the section."

- **Formatting and Structure**: It can suggest ways to improve document structure, such as adding headings, creating bullet points, or offering design layout suggestions.

Microsoft Excel

- **Data Analysis**: Copilot helps with real-time data analysis. For example, if you have a spreadsheet full of raw data, Copilot can suggest trends, patterns, and insights based on the numbers.

- **Formula Suggestions**: Copilot can offer formula suggestions and assist in troubleshooting errors in existing formulas. If you type something like "sum these values," it will suggest an appropriate function.

- **Chart and Graph Recommendations**: As you work with data, Copilot can recommend charts or graphs that best represent the data you're working with, such as line graphs for trends or bar charts for comparisons.

Microsoft PowerPoint

- **Slide Creation**: While working on a presentation, Copilot can help generate slides based on text or bullet points. It can even suggest slide layouts or formatting.

- **Design Ideas**: Copilot can recommend design adjustments, such as color schemes, font styles, and visual themes that match the content of your slides.

- **Real-Time Editing**: If you're editing a slide, Copilot may suggest ways to improve visual hierarchy or ensure that text fits neatly into the slide layout.

Microsoft Outlook

- **Email Composition**: Copilot provides suggestions for drafting emails. For example, it might suggest a more concise way to phrase a sentence, improve email tone, or help you quickly draft a response to a received email.

- **Summarizing Email Threads**: If you're dealing with a long email thread, Copilot can offer a summary of the key points, helping you quickly get up to speed on the conversation.

- **Scheduling Assistance**: Copilot can suggest meeting times or help you manage your calendar by suggesting available time slots for meetings based on your schedule.

Microsoft Teams

- **Meeting Summaries**: After a meeting, Copilot can generate a summary, highlighting key decisions, action items, and deadlines.

- **Task Assignment**: Copilot can assist in organizing and assigning tasks in real time, ensuring everyone knows their responsibilities post-meeting.

- **Response Suggestions**: While participating in chat conversations, Copilot may suggest quick replies or assist in drafting messages based on the ongoing conversation.

3. Using Real-Time Suggestions Effectively

- **Natural Language Inputs**: Simply type requests in natural language, and Copilot will interpret them and offer suggestions. For instance:

  - In Word: "Rewrite this paragraph to sound more professional."

  - In Excel: "Show trends in this data over the past five years."

  - In Outlook: "Draft a follow-up email for this client."

- **Interact with Suggestions**: When Copilot suggests something, you can accept it, reject it, or refine it further. It's designed to be flexible and adjust based on your feedback.

- **Prompt Refinement**: If a suggestion isn't quite right, you can refine your prompt. For instance, if you're not happy with a summary, you can ask for more detail or a different tone.

4. Contextual and Collaborative Suggestions

- **Collaborative Work**: Copilot assists in collaborative settings. For example, in a shared Word document, Copilot may suggest improvements to both your content and formatting, ensuring that your document is consistent with the team's tone and style.

- **Group Discussions**: In Teams or collaborative projects, Copilot can suggest real-time responses based on previous interactions or ongoing conversations.

- **Real-Time Editing Suggestions**: As you and others make changes in real time, Copilot offers suggestions that keep everyone on the same page, ensuring consistency and smooth workflows.

5. Adjusting Copilot's Real-Time Feedback

- **Refining Output**: Depending on your preferences, you can ask Copilot to refine its suggestions. If you're working on formal writing, you can instruct Copilot to maintain a professional tone, or if you're writing creatively, you can adjust the style accordingly.

- **Turn Off Suggestions**: If at any point you find the suggestions distracting, you can turn off real-time suggestions in the settings of the app you are using.

6. Benefits of Real-Time Assistance and Suggestions

- **Time-Saving**: Copilot's suggestions help you save time by automating repetitive tasks, improving document quality, and analyzing data quickly.

- **Enhanced Accuracy**: With Copilot offering real-time suggestions, your documents, emails, and data are more likely to be accurate, well-structured, and error-free.

- **Improved Collaboration**: When working in teams, Copilot ensures that suggestions are aligned with team preferences, making collaboration smoother and more efficient.

7. Providing Feedback for Improvement

- Copilot uses machine learning to improve its suggestions over time. If you notice something that doesn't quite fit, you can provide feedback directly within the app, helping to fine-tune its responses.

With real-time assistance and suggestions, Microsoft Copilot becomes a powerful tool to streamline tasks and enhance productivity. It adapts to your workflow, providing the right suggestions at the right time, allowing you to focus on the content and strategic decisions rather than repetitive tasks.

Integration with Microsoft 365

Microsoft Copilot is deeply integrated into Microsoft 365, providing seamless assistance across a wide range of applications such as Word, Excel, PowerPoint, Outlook, and Teams. This integration enhances productivity by leveraging AI capabilities directly within the Microsoft 365 environment, ensuring that users can access real-time support and intelligent suggestions wherever they are working.

Here's how Copilot integrates with various Microsoft 365 apps:

Copilot

Microsoft 365 Personal and Family now includes AI

The Microsoft 365 you know and love is better than ever before, with new AI-powered features.[1]

1. Microsoft Word

- **Document Creation and Editing**: Copilot assists with creating and editing documents by suggesting content, generating summaries, improving sentence structure, and helping with formatting.

  - **Content Suggestions**: Copilot can generate paragraphs, suggest rewording, or even help create content based on specific prompts. You can ask it to draft emails, reports, or essays by simply entering a command like "Write a professional email summarizing the project."

  - **Formatting Help**: Copilot can suggest and apply formatting improvements to ensure your document is well-organized and visually appealing.

- **Integration Example**: If you are drafting a proposal in Word, Copilot might suggest relevant content from your past documents, helping you save time. It can also provide style and tone recommendations.

2. Microsoft Excel

- **Data Analysis**: Copilot enhances data analysis by suggesting formulas, generating charts, summarizing trends, and even creating pivot tables.

  - **Formula Suggestions**: You can ask Copilot to assist with complex formulas, or even suggest the right function (e.g., SUMIF, VLOOKUP) based on your data.

  - **Data Visualization**: Copilot can recommend and generate visualizations like charts, graphs, and data tables to present your data more effectively.

- **Integration Example**: When working with sales data, you can ask Copilot, "What are the sales trends over the last quarter?" Copilot will generate a trend analysis and suggest relevant graphs.

3. Microsoft PowerPoint

- **Slide Creation and Design**: Copilot helps create and design presentations. It can generate slides from bullet points, suggest slide layouts, and recommend design improvements.

  - **Content Generation**: You can enter a prompt such as "Create a presentation on climate change," and Copilot will generate slides with appropriate text and images.

  - **Design Recommendations**: Copilot can also recommend design elements like colours, fonts, and layouts to improve the overall appearance and impact of your presentation.

- **Integration Example**: If you're presenting quarterly results, Copilot will pull relevant data from Excel and automatically generate slides, helping you visualize the key points.

4. Microsoft Outlook

- **Email Composition**: Copilot assists in drafting emails, summarizing conversations, and suggesting replies. It can generate professional-sounding email responses based on your prompts, saving you time and effort.

  - **Summarizing Threads**: Copilot can provide quick summaries of long email threads, helping you stay on top of important communications.

- o **Drafting Responses**: You can ask Copilot to write responses such as "Follow up with this client" or "Thank you for the update," and it will generate a draft that you can send.

- **Integration Example**: When you receive an email from a client, you can instruct Copilot to "Draft a polite follow-up email" or "Summarize this conversation," and Copilot will generate the email for you, considering the context of the thread.

5. Microsoft Teams

- **Meeting Summaries**: Copilot provides automatic meeting summaries, highlighting key discussion points, action items, and deadlines. It can be particularly useful in team meetings where multiple topics are discussed.

  - o **Task Creation**: Copilot can help assign tasks to team members based on meeting outcomes. For instance, it can create tasks directly in Teams or integrate with project management tools like Planner or To Do.

  - o **Real-Time Collaboration**: Copilot assists during live chat or video calls by suggesting quick responses, summarizing discussions, and providing real-time data analysis.

- **Integration Example**: After a meeting, Copilot can generate a summary with key takeaways and action items, which you can share directly in the Teams channel for everyone to access.

6. OneNote

- **Note-Taking Assistance**: Copilot can help organize notes, extract key points from meeting notes or brainstorming sessions, and suggest ways to structure your notes more effectively.

  - o **Content Organization**: Copilot can automatically organize notes by topic, date, or relevance, making it easier to navigate your notes.

- **Integration Example**: While you're taking notes in a team meeting, Copilot can suggest adding headings, subheadings, and even tagging important sections for future reference.

7. Microsoft Search and OneDrive

- **Search Integration**: Copilot integrates with Microsoft Search, allowing you to ask it to find specific documents, emails, or files across your organization or OneDrive.

  - o **Contextual Search**: Copilot can search not only by file name but also by the content within documents. For example, you can ask, "Find all documents related to the marketing strategy," and Copilot will pull up relevant documents.

- **Integration Example**: If you need a specific contract document, you can ask Copilot, "Find the contract I worked on last month," and it will search OneDrive or SharePoint for the relevant document.

8. Power Automate and Other Microsoft 365 Tools

- **Automation**: Copilot integrates with Power Automate to help automate workflows. It can help create automated tasks based on user input or recurring actions. For example, it might suggest automating the process of sending reminders about meetings or deadlines.

- **Integration with SharePoint**: If your organization uses SharePoint, Copilot can suggest ways to organize or find information within SharePoint sites, making collaboration easier.

9. Third-Party App Integrations

- **Custom Integration**: Microsoft Copilot can integrate with third-party applications that you use within the Microsoft ecosystem. For example, it might work with tools like Salesforce or LinkedIn to pull in relevant information about clients or leads and assist with communication, reporting, or presentation.

- **Integration Example**: While working in Excel, Copilot can suggest pulling in customer data from Salesforce and analysing it to identify trends or sales opportunities.

10. Security and Compliance Integration

- **Data Protection**: Copilot ensures that all suggestions and integrations comply with your organization's security and privacy policies, leveraging Microsoft's security infrastructure.

- **Compliance Features**: Copilot's integration follows Microsoft's compliance framework, making sure that data is handled appropriately within the legal and regulatory context of your region or industry.

How to Make the Most of Microsoft Copilot's Integration

- **Consistency Across Apps**: Since Copilot is integrated across Microsoft 365 apps, it provides a consistent experience. You can switch between Word, Excel, and Teams without losing context, ensuring that you stay productive across multiple tools.

- **Custom Commands**: Create custom commands or templates based on your team's needs. For example, if your team often generates project reports, you can create a template in Word or PowerPoint where Copilot automatically fills in key details.

- **Learning Over Time**: Copilot learns from your interactions over time, improving its suggestions and responses as it gets more context from your work.

By integrating seamlessly into your workflow across Microsoft 365, Copilot ensures that your productivity is enhanced with AI-driven insights, suggestions, and automation.

AI-Powered Insights and Analytics

AI-Powered Insights and Analytics in Microsoft Copilot provide valuable data-driven recommendations, patterns, and visualizations that can greatly enhance decision-making and productivity across various applications within Microsoft 365.

These AI-driven capabilities enable users to analyse data, generate reports, and receive actionable insights in real-time, making it easier to work smarter and optimize workflows.

Here's how AI-Powered Insights and Analytics work across different Microsoft 365 applications:

1. Microsoft Excel

- **Data Analysis**: Copilot can help you analyse large datasets by detecting patterns and trends, providing predictive insights that would otherwise require advanced data analysis skills.

- o **Trend Identification**: Based on the data, Copilot can automatically identify trends (e.g., sales growth, declining revenue) and present them in an easy-to-understand format such as graphs or charts.

  - o **What-If Analysis**: Copilot can perform scenario analysis, helping you explore various outcomes by changing certain variables within your data. For example, if you're working with a sales forecast, Copilot can analyse how different sales strategies could affect revenue.

  - o **Automated Insights**: Copilot can generate insights such as "Top 10 customers by revenue" or "Largest cost drivers for the quarter" with a click of a button, streamlining complex data analysis tasks.

- **Integration Example**: If you have a dataset with employee performance metrics, Copilot can automatically analyse performance across different departments and highlight key areas needing improvement or recognize top performers.

2. Microsoft Power BI

- **Interactive Dashboards**: Copilot can integrate with **Power BI** to enhance dashboards with AI-generated insights. It helps visualize complex data points, making the information easier to digest and act upon.

  - o **Advanced Analytics**: Copilot can help uncover hidden patterns or correlations in your data using machine learning algorithms.

  - o **Smart Suggestions**: Power BI integrated with Copilot provides intelligent recommendations for visualizations based on the data you're working with. For example, if you're analysing customer data, Copilot may suggest a segmentation report or customer lifetime value analysis.

  - o **Natural Language Queries**: You can use natural language to ask questions like "What is the sales performance for this region?" or "Which product category has the highest growth this quarter?" Copilot will interpret your request and generate relevant reports.

- **Integration Example**: If you're tracking monthly sales performance, Copilot will suggest automatic charts and graphs that visualize the data in a way that highlights the key insights, such as sales spikes or trends over time.

3. Microsoft Word

- **Content Analysis and Summarization**: Copilot in Word analyses your written content and provides feedback, such as readability scores, tone analysis, and recommendations for improvements.

  - o **Style Recommendations**: Based on AI-driven analysis, Copilot might suggest adjusting the writing style to match your intended tone, whether it's formal, informal, persuasive, or neutral.

  - o **Automated Summaries**: If you're dealing with long documents, Copilot can generate concise summaries that capture the key points, saving you time on reading lengthy materials.

- **Integration Example**: If you're drafting a business proposal, Copilot will not only suggest content improvements but also provide feedback on the document's tone, ensuring that the message aligns with professional standards.

4. Microsoft Teams

- **Meeting Insights**: After a meeting, Copilot can generate actionable insights by summarizing key discussion points, decisions, and action items.

  - **Meeting Summaries**: AI analyzes the conversation, creating a structured summary with all key details, ensuring that you don't miss any important discussions or follow-ups.

  - **Sentiment Analysis**: Copilot can gauge the overall sentiment of the conversation in Teams chats or meetings, helping you understand how employees feel about specific topics or projects.

- **Integration Example**: After a project meeting, Copilot can analyze the conversation and provide insights like "80% of the team agrees on the proposed timeline" or "Concern raised about resource allocation."

5. Microsoft Outlook

- **Email Analytics**: Copilot can help analyze your email communication patterns and offer suggestions for improving efficiency, clarity, and tone.

  - **Response Time Insights**: Copilot can analyze how quickly you typically respond to emails and suggest improvements, such as setting reminders for follow-up or flagging emails requiring urgent responses.

  - **Sender/Recipient Insights**: Copilot may analyze communication frequency with contacts, providing recommendations for improving email flow and reducing back-and-forth messages.

- **Integration Example**: Copilot can help summarize your daily emails, flagging the most important ones and even suggesting responses based on past communication styles.

6. Microsoft OneDrive and SharePoint

- **Document Insights**: Copilot analyzes documents stored in **OneDrive** or **SharePoint** and provides insights such as most viewed documents, trends in document usage, or collaboration statistics.

  - **Collaboration Trends**: Copilot can identify who is interacting with your documents the most and provide insights into the level of collaboration and document sharing.

  - **Content Suggestions**: Based on the document you're working on, Copilot can recommend related files, making it easier to find relevant content stored across your organization.

- **Integration Example**: If you're working on a project proposal, Copilot can suggest related documents in SharePoint and provide insights on how often certain documents were accessed by the team.

7. Power Automate

- **Automated Analytics**: Copilot can analyze your workflows created in **Power Automate** and suggest ways to improve process efficiency.

  - o **Workflow Insights**: Copilot can analyze your automated processes and offer recommendations on streamlining repetitive tasks or improving automation efficiency.

  - o **Predictive Insights**: Copilot uses AI to predict bottlenecks or areas where the process might fail, helping you proactively improve your workflows.

- **Integration Example**: If you have an automated workflow for employee onboarding, Copilot can provide insights on how long each step takes, and suggest improvements to reduce delays.

8. Security and Compliance Insights

- **Security Analytics**: Copilot integrates with Microsoft's security tools to provide real-time analytics on potential risks and threats within your documents or emails.

  - o **Data Loss Prevention**: Copilot can identify any sensitive information in documents or emails, helping you ensure compliance with data protection laws like GDPR.

  - o **Compliance Monitoring**: Copilot offers insights into compliance trends across your organization and suggests areas where more robust security measures may be needed.

- **Integration Example**: Copilot can alert you if a document contains personally identifiable information (PII) that violates your organization's compliance policies.

9. Cross-App Insights

- **Data Correlation**: Copilot allows you to correlate data across apps within Microsoft 365. For instance, you can analyze data from Excel, meetings in Teams, and emails in Outlook to generate deeper insights.

  - o **Contextual Recommendations**: Copilot can use information from one app to suggest actions in another. For example, after analyzing data in Excel, it might recommend sending a summary report via email in Outlook or presenting the results in PowerPoint.

- **Integration Example**: If you're working on a quarterly report in Excel, Copilot might recommend turning your findings into a presentation in PowerPoint, based on the insights it gathers.

How to Make the Most of AI-Powered Insights and Analytics:

1. **Leverage Natural Language**: You can interact with Copilot using natural language queries. Ask questions like, "What trends can I identify from this data?" or "Summarize the findings from my last meeting," and Copilot will provide data-driven insights.

2. **Data-Driven Decisions**: Use AI-powered insights to make informed, data-backed decisions in real-time. For instance, Copilot can help you optimize business strategies based on customer data or sales trends.

3. **Optimize Workflows**: Copilot can identify inefficiencies and recommend optimizations to improve workflow, data management, and collaboration efforts across your team.

4. **Monitor Project Progress**: Copilot offers real-time analytics and summaries of project data, helping you stay on track with deadlines and goals.

5. **Customizable Dashboards**: In tools like Power BI, customize your dashboards to track the metrics that matter most to your team or organization, and let Copilot surface insights based on those metrics.

AI-powered insights and analytics in Microsoft Copilot transform how you interact with data, make decisions, and manage your workflow, making Microsoft 365 an even more powerful tool for productivity and efficiency.

Automation of Repetitive Tasks

Automation of Repetitive Tasks with Microsoft Copilot within Microsoft 365 helps you streamline workflows, save time, and reduce manual effort. By leveraging AI-powered automation, you can eliminate routine tasks and focus on more strategic or creative aspects of your work. This is made possible through various tools like **Power Automate**, **Excel**, **Teams**, and **Outlook**, all integrated with Copilot to help you automate repetitive actions.

Here's how **Copilot** helps in automating tasks across different Microsoft 365 applications:

1. Microsoft Power Automate

- **Automating Workflows**: Power Automate (formerly Microsoft Flow) allows you to create automated workflows for common tasks. With Copilot, you can easily build workflows without needing extensive technical skills.

  - **Templates**: Copilot can suggest pre-built templates for automating tasks like sending notifications, updating records, or transferring files across different platforms (SharePoint, OneDrive, Outlook, etc.).

  - **Triggered Actions**: Copilot can help you set up triggers for actions, such as sending an email when a specific condition is met (e.g., a new document is uploaded to SharePoint, or a new lead is entered into your CRM).

  - **Integration with Third-Party Apps**: Copilot allows seamless integration between Microsoft 365 and external services like Salesforce, Slack, Trello, and others, enabling cross-platform automation.

- **Integration Example**: Set up a workflow where, when a new project is added to **Trello**, a corresponding task is created in **Planner**, and a notification is sent via **Teams** to the relevant team members.

2. Microsoft Excel

- **Automating Data Entry and Analysis**: Copilot can assist in automating data processing tasks in Excel by suggesting macros or formulas that save time on repetitive calculations and reporting.

  - **Predefined Templates**: Copilot can suggest templates for recurring reports, such as monthly sales reports or inventory tracking, and automatically populate them based on your data.

- **Formula Automation**: Copilot can automate complex formulas, ensuring that data across columns or sheets is updated without manual intervention. For example, a recurring sales report could be automatically populated every week with the latest figures.

- **Data Validation**: Copilot can be set to validate or clean data regularly (e.g., removing duplicates, correcting formats), eliminating manual oversight.

- **Integration Example**: If you track expenses in Excel, Copilot can create a recurring workflow to update the data every month and send you a reminder to approve the entries.

3. Microsoft Outlook

- **Email Management Automation**: Copilot can assist in automating tasks like managing your inbox, responding to emails, and scheduling meetings.

  - **Automated Email Replies**: Copilot can create custom automatic replies for certain types of emails, such as vacation responses, or set up recurring email sequences for outreach and follow-up.

  - **Folder Organization**: Copilot can sort incoming emails into appropriate folders based on subject, sender, or keywords, keeping your inbox organized without you having to do it manually.

  - **Scheduling Tasks**: Copilot can also schedule reminders for you to follow up on certain emails, set up meetings, or complete tasks based on email content.

- **Integration Example**: Copilot can read incoming client emails, automatically generate a draft response based on the content, and even schedule meetings directly in **Teams** or **Outlook**.

4. Microsoft Teams

- **Meeting Scheduling and Management**: Copilot can automate scheduling, summarizing, and following up on meetings.

  - **Automated Scheduling**: Copilot can help set up meetings based on participants' availability, suggest optimal times, and create calendar events with necessary information.

  - **Automated Reminders and Alerts**: It can send out meeting reminders to participants and alert you of upcoming deadlines, helping keep teams on track.

  - **Follow-Up and Task Creation**: After meetings, Copilot can create tasks from action items discussed and send follow-up emails to participants with important notes or next steps.

- **Integration Example**: Copilot can schedule recurring standup meetings every Monday morning, send reminders to the team about the agenda, and even follow up with action points after each meeting.

5. Microsoft Word

- **Document Creation**: Copilot can help automate document generation, especially when creating documents with repetitive content or structures, like reports, proposals, or contracts.

- **Template Usage**: Copilot can suggest or create document templates based on previous documents you've worked on, saving time on layout and formatting.

- **Auto-Fill Content**: If you frequently generate reports based on specific data or sources, Copilot can auto-fill sections of the document with the appropriate content, such as market data, statistics, or client details.

- **Repetitive Formatting**: If you work with documents requiring consistent formatting (e.g., headings, styles, citations), Copilot can apply these consistently without manual intervention.

- **Integration Example**: If you create quarterly business reports, Copilot can automatically pull in the latest data from **Excel** and generate a new report for you in **Word**, formatted and ready to go.

6. Microsoft SharePoint

- **Automating Document Management**: Copilot can help automate document management tasks like file uploads, version control, and approval workflows in **SharePoint**.

  - **Automated Document Filing**: It can automatically categorize and tag documents based on their content, saving you from having to organize files manually.

  - **Approval Workflows**: Copilot can create automated workflows for document approval, ensuring that the right team members review documents at the appropriate stages.

- **Integration Example**: When a new document is uploaded to **SharePoint**, Copilot can automatically route it to the correct team for approval and send reminders to reviewers.

7. Microsoft OneDrive

- **Automating File Backup and Syncing**: Copilot can manage the automatic syncing and backup of your files across devices, ensuring that files are always up to date without manual intervention.

  - **File Organization**: It can help organize your files into predefined folders or categories, keeping your OneDrive neat and accessible.

- **Integration Example**: Copilot can set up a rule to automatically upload new files from your desktop to a specific OneDrive folder and even organize them by type (e.g., presentations, documents, spreadsheets).

8. Microsoft Planner

- **Task Assignment and Tracking**: Copilot can automate task creation and assignment within **Planner**, ensuring that tasks are assigned to the right people at the right time.

  - **Recurring Tasks**: Copilot can set up recurring tasks, such as weekly check-ins or monthly reports, and automatically assign them to the appropriate team members.

  - **Progress Monitoring**: Copilot can monitor task progress and alert you when deadlines are approaching, ensuring that tasks are completed on time.

- **Integration Example**: For project management, Copilot can generate weekly status reports from **Planner** and send them to the project manager automatically.

9. Microsoft To Do

- **Task List Automation**: Copilot can help automate the management of your to-do list by adding, categorizing, and prioritizing tasks.

  - **Task Creation**: Copilot can automatically add tasks to your list based on emails, meeting notes, or calendar events. For example, it can automatically create a task from a meeting action item or an email request.

  - **Recurring Tasks**: Set up recurring tasks for regular activities such as team check-ins, reporting, or document review.

- **Integration Example**: Copilot can analyze your upcoming meetings and automatically generate action items as tasks in **To Do** for follow-up.

How to Get the Most Out of Task Automation with Copilot:

1. **Integrate Across Apps**: Utilize **Power Automate** to connect tasks across Microsoft 365 apps, ensuring that when a task happens in one app, it triggers an action in another.

2. **Create Custom Automations**: Set up custom workflows tailored to your specific needs. For example, automate the process of archiving emails after they've been responded to, or create a task in Planner when a project document is updated.

3. **Use Templates**: Leverage pre-built templates in **Power Automate** to kickstart your automation journey, then modify them to suit your workflow.

4. **Regularly Review and Optimize**: Periodically assess your automated workflows to ensure they remain efficient and update them as your processes evolve.

5. **Combine AI with Automation**: Use Copilot's AI-driven suggestions and insights to continually improve your automated workflows. For example, Copilot can suggest ways to streamline a repetitive process based on usage patterns.

By leveraging **Microsoft Copilot** and **Power Automate**, you can significantly reduce the time spent on repetitive tasks, boost productivity, and ensure that your work processes are more efficient and automated across Microsoft 365 applications.

Natural Language Processing Capabilities

Natural Language Processing (NLP) Capabilities in **Microsoft Copilot** enhance the way users interact with their Microsoft 365 applications by allowing the system to understand, interpret, and generate human language in a natural and intuitive manner.

This enables a range of powerful features that can streamline workflows, enhance productivity, and improve user experience across various tasks.

Here's how **NLP capabilities** in **Copilot** enhance Microsoft 365 tools:

1. Text Generation and Summarization

- **Automatic Summaries**: Copilot can quickly analyze long documents, emails, or meeting notes and generate concise summaries, saving you time by highlighting key points and critical information.

- **Content Generation**: Using NLP, Copilot can assist in drafting emails, reports, or other documents based on a brief or topic you provide. It can generate coherent text, suggest improvements, or even write entire sections based on existing content.

Example: In **Word**, Copilot can summarize a lengthy report or meeting transcript into a few key points or generate a detailed summary based on your preferred length.

2. Language Understanding and Commands

- **Voice and Text Commands**: Copilot can understand natural language commands, allowing you to interact with your Microsoft apps using simple, conversational language.

  - **Voice-to-Text**: With integrated voice recognition, you can speak directly to Copilot to execute tasks like scheduling meetings, sending emails, or opening files.

  - **Text-Based Commands**: You can type commands in plain language (e.g., "Create a new presentation based on the attached document") and Copilot will interpret and act on it.

Example: In **Outlook**, you can ask Copilot, "Summarize the email thread from yesterday" or "Create a task from this email" and Copilot will respond with the necessary actions.

3. Context-Aware Responses

- **Contextual Understanding**: Copilot can understand the context of your work, whether you are writing a report, preparing a presentation, or analyzing data, and offer suggestions accordingly. It adapts to your language style, tone, and content to provide relevant input.

- **Dynamic Suggestions**: Copilot offers intelligent suggestions based on the document or task you are working on. For example, it can suggest a phrase, reword a sentence for clarity, or offer a statistical insight based on the data at hand.

Example: In **Excel**, Copilot can interpret the data you are working with and offer insights like, "Would you like me to analyse trends in this data?" or "Here's a summary of your data with potential outliers."

4. Sentiment Analysis

- **Analysing Tone and Sentiment**: Copilot uses NLP to detect the sentiment in documents, emails, or messages. It can identify whether the tone is positive, negative, or neutral and offer suggestions on improving the tone or making communication clearer and more effective.

Example: In **Outlook**, Copilot can analyze an email you are drafting and suggest making it more polite or assertive, depending on the context. It can also suggest rephrasing if the tone seems too aggressive or too casual.

5. Language Translation and Localization

- **Real-Time Translation**: Copilot can automatically translate text between multiple languages, making it easier to collaborate with international teams or understand documents written in different languages.

- **Localization**: Copilot understands cultural nuances and can adapt content to suit regional differences in tone, terminology, or phrasing.

Example: In **Teams**, if a participant is speaking in another language, Copilot can provide real-time translations, ensuring smooth communication across diverse teams.

6. Intelligent Search and Query Processing

- **Natural Language Search**: Copilot enhances search functionality across Microsoft 365 apps by enabling natural language queries. You can ask questions in plain language, and Copilot will return relevant results from your documents, emails, calendars, and more.

Example: In **OneDrive**, you can search for a file using a phrase like, "Find the project proposal from last month," and Copilot will show relevant documents based on that context, even if the file name doesn't exactly match.

7. Email and Document Categorization

- **Smart Categorization**: Copilot can analyze your incoming emails and documents and categorize them automatically based on their content, urgency, or relevance.

    - **Email Sorting**: Copilot can categorize emails by priority or topic (e.g., "Important," "Action Required," "Low Priority") and sort them accordingly in **Outlook**.

    - **Document Classification**: It can classify documents based on their content type (e.g., contracts, reports, proposals) and even suggest relevant folders in **OneDrive** or **SharePoint** for storage.

Example: In **SharePoint**, Copilot can tag documents with specific keywords and organize them based on the subject matter, ensuring you find the content you need quickly.

8. Enhanced Collaboration in Teams

- **Intelligent Chatbots**: Copilot's NLP capabilities can power intelligent chatbots within **Microsoft Teams**, allowing you to interact with bots to answer questions, complete tasks, or retrieve information from shared files.

- **Automatic Meeting Notes**: During meetings in **Teams**, Copilot can take notes, summarize discussions, and highlight key action items using NLP.

Example: During a **Teams** meeting, Copilot can provide real-time captions and also summarize the discussion afterward, highlighting important points and action items.

9. Content Insights and Recommendations

- **Content Analysis**: Copilot can analyze the content in documents, presentations, and spreadsheets and provide insights or recommendations to improve them.

- o **Document Editing**: It can suggest improvements for grammar, style, and structure, as well as recommend key points to add or remove.

- o **Presentation Recommendations**: In **PowerPoint**, Copilot can recommend design improvements, suggest content to enhance your slides, and even help with content formatting based on the document's context.

Example: Copilot in **PowerPoint** might suggest adding more visuals to a slide to better convey your message or offer a different layout to improve clarity and engagement.

10. Customizable Language Models

- **Tailored Models**: Copilot allows for customizable language models to match your company's tone, style, and specific needs. This makes interactions more personalized, ensuring that the system adapts to your unique way of working and communicating.

Example: If you work in customer service, Copilot can be trained to generate responses that match the tone and language style typically used in customer communications, ensuring consistency across all interactions.

How to Leverage NLP Capabilities in Microsoft Copilot:

1. **Use Natural Language to Save Time**: Instead of manually searching for files or composing emails, use plain language to interact with Copilot. It can interpret your requests and execute tasks for you.

2. **Optimize Document Creation**: Utilize Copilot's text generation and summarization features to quickly draft documents or emails, saving time on manual writing and editing.

3. **Collaborate Seamlessly**: In **Teams**, let Copilot take meeting notes, summarize discussions, and provide recommendations for follow-up tasks, ensuring smoother and more efficient collaboration.

4. **Improve Communication**: Use Copilot's sentiment analysis and tone recommendations to improve the clarity and tone of your emails, ensuring more effective and professional communication.

5. **Stay Organized**: Let Copilot categorize your emails, documents, and tasks, ensuring that you stay on top of important activities and deadlines.

By integrating **NLP capabilities**, **Microsoft Copilot** elevates productivity across the **Microsoft 365** ecosystem, helping you work more efficiently with language-based tasks such as writing, summarizing, searching, and collaborating. These features transform the way users interact with their digital workspace, making complex tasks easier and more intuitive.

CHAPTER FOUR
<u>USING MICROSOFT COPILOT IN DIFFERENT APPLICATIONS</u>

<u>Microsoft Word</u>

Microsoft Word is one of the most widely used word-processing applications within the **Microsoft 365** suite, and with **Microsoft Copilot** integrated, it offers powerful AI-driven tools to enhance productivity and streamline document creation.

Copilot can assist in a variety of tasks, from drafting documents to generating summaries, improving grammar, and offering real-time suggestions based on the content you are working with.

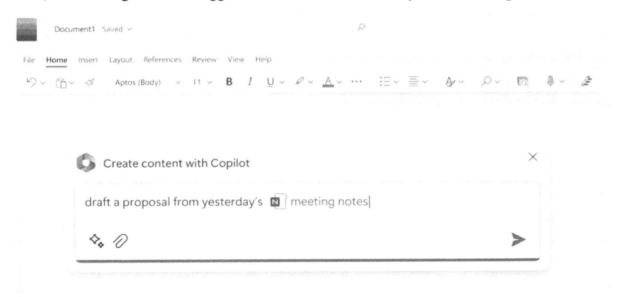

1. Content Creation and Drafting

- **Text Generation**: Copilot can assist in generating text for your document based on a brief or topic you provide. Whether you are creating a report, essay, proposal, or letter, Copilot can provide coherent, contextually relevant paragraphs.

  - **Example**: You could type, "Create an introduction for a report on market trends," and Copilot will generate an appropriate introductory paragraph based on the context and data you have provided.

- **Auto-Completion of Sentences**: Copilot can help finish sentences or suggest the next phrase based on what you've typed, speeding up document creation and ensuring a more natural flow of ideas.

  - **Example**: If you start a sentence with "The primary objective of this report is to...", Copilot might suggest the rest of the sentence based on the context of the report.

2. Summarization and Condensing Information

- **Automatic Summaries**: Copilot can summarize long documents, articles, or research papers, extracting key points and condensing the text into shorter, more digestible summaries.

- **Example**: If you're working with a lengthy report, you can ask Copilot, "Summarize the main points of this document," and it will create a condensed version focusing on the key insights.

- **Highlighting Key Information**: Copilot can automatically identify and highlight important information or actionable items in a document. This helps you quickly focus on what matters most in your content.

3. Grammar, Spelling, and Style Improvements

- **Grammar and Spell Check**: Copilot offers real-time suggestions for correcting spelling, grammar, and punctuation errors, ensuring that your document is professional and polished.

  - **Example**: If you accidentally type "There is many options," Copilot will suggest "There are many options," correcting the grammatical mistake automatically.

- **Style Recommendations**: Copilot can assess the writing style of your document and suggest improvements. For instance, it can help make your tone more formal or casual depending on the context of your document.

  - **Example**: If you are writing a business proposal, Copilot might recommend adjusting the tone to sound more formal or assertive, ensuring that your writing aligns with professional standards.

4. Content Optimization

- **Clarity and Readability Enhancements**: Copilot can help you improve the clarity of your document by suggesting simpler words or rephrasing sentences to make them more readable.

  - **Example**: If you've written a complex sentence, Copilot might suggest breaking it down into two simpler sentences or recommending a more straightforward word choice.

- **Keyword Suggestions**: If you're writing SEO-driven content or trying to improve the focus of your document, Copilot can suggest keywords or phrases to include based on the context.

  - **Example**: While writing an article on digital marketing, Copilot might suggest keywords like "SEO," "PPC," or "content strategy" to enhance the relevance of your document.

5. Design and Layout Assistance

- **Smart Formatting**: Copilot can help automatically format your document by adjusting headings, bullet points, and text alignment to improve the overall structure.

  - **Example**: If you're writing a report and have large blocks of text, Copilot might suggest breaking it up into smaller paragraphs or adding a table of contents based on the content structure.

- **Document Design Suggestions**: Copilot can recommend design elements like font styles, colours, and layout improvements that will make your document look more professional and visually appealing.

  - **Example**: If you're creating a presentation-style report in Word, Copilot might suggest appropriate themes or layouts to enhance the document's visual appeal.

6. Data and Content Integration

- **Excel and Data Integration**: If you are working with data or tables in your Word document, Copilot can help you import data from **Excel** or **Power BI** and insert it seamlessly into your document.

  - **Example**: If you need to include a table or chart from **Excel**, Copilot can insert it into Word and ensure it's formatted appropriately, making it easy to integrate detailed information into your document.

- **Dynamic Tables and Charts**: Copilot can assist in generating dynamic tables and charts, which will update automatically if the underlying data changes.

  - **Example**: If you're writing a financial report and want to include a chart or table, Copilot can pull data from **Excel** and insert an up-to-date chart that reflects the current numbers.

7. Collaboration and Commenting

- **Real-time Collaboration**: With **Word** in Microsoft 365, you can collaborate on documents in real-time with colleagues. Copilot can help streamline this process by suggesting edits or responding to comments automatically.

  - **Example**: If multiple people are editing a document, Copilot can highlight suggested changes in real-time and allow you to accept or reject them.

- **Comment and Action Item Generation**: Copilot can create action items or highlight comments from collaborators, ensuring that no important feedback is missed.

  - **Example**: In a collaborative report, Copilot can extract comments made by others and summarize them for quick review.

8. Custom Templates and Content Personalization

- **Template Generation**: Copilot can help you create custom templates for recurring documents. Based on your past documents, it can suggest a format or layout that suits the type of document you're creating.

  - **Example**: If you frequently create client proposals, Copilot can offer a proposal template tailored to your specific industry, with sections for introduction, goals, budget, and timeline.

- **Personalized Suggestions**: Copilot can tailor its suggestions based on your writing habits, offering personalized recommendations that match your style, tone, and preferred formats.

9. Language and Translation Tools

- **Language Translation**: Copilot can assist in translating text from one language to another, making it easier to create multilingual documents or work with international teams.

  - **Example**: If you need to translate a report from English to Spanish, Copilot can provide accurate translation suggestions or even translate the document automatically.

- **Multilingual Support**: Copilot's language understanding enables it to seamlessly work with documents in multiple languages, adjusting its suggestions based on the document's language.

10. Real-Time Feedback

- **Instant Editing Suggestions**: Copilot offers feedback as you type, giving you instant suggestions for improvement or corrections.

    o **Example**: If you're writing a formal letter and use casual language, Copilot might suggest more professional alternatives in real time.

- **Writing Assistance**: Copilot can provide specific advice based on your document's content, such as recommending additional information, rephrasing a sentence for clarity, or suggesting a more effective conclusion.

How to Leverage Microsoft Word with Copilot:

1. **Start with a Template**: If you're working on a report or proposal, start with a Copilot-recommended template that matches your document's structure, saving time on formatting.

2. **Collaborate in Real-Time**: Use **Microsoft Word**'s collaborative features with **Copilot** to streamline the editing and review process, ensuring you can quickly address feedback.

3. **Use for Research**: Let Copilot help you summarize research papers or articles and generate key insights for your own writing.

4. **Ensure Consistency**: Utilize Copilot's grammar and style improvement features to ensure your document maintains consistency in tone, language, and format.

5. **Incorporate Data and Charts**: Easily integrate and visualize data by pulling from **Excel** or **Power BI**, letting Copilot format it appropriately for your document.

By integrating **Microsoft Copilot** into **Microsoft Word**, you can create more professional, error-free, and compelling documents faster. Whether you're drafting, summarizing, or collaborating, Copilot helps enhance your productivity and efficiency.

Microsoft Excel

Microsoft Excel, as part of the **Microsoft 365** suite, is a powerful tool for data analysis, organization, and visualization. With the integration of **Microsoft Copilot**, Excel becomes even more efficient and intelligent, providing AI-driven insights, automation, and enhanced capabilities for tasks like data entry, analysis, and reporting.

Here's how **Microsoft Copilot** can transform your Excel experience:

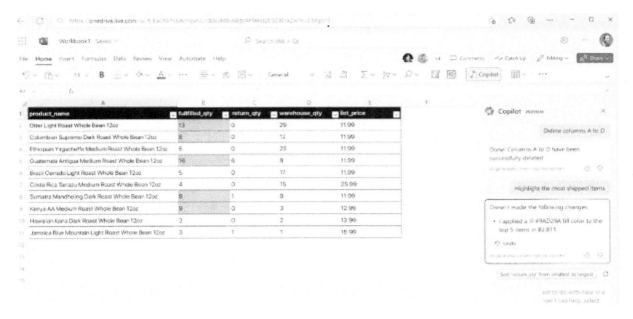

1. Data Insights and Analysis

- **Automatic Insights**: Copilot can analyse your data and offer valuable insights, identifying trends, outliers, and patterns without you needing to run complex formulas manually.

    o **Example**: If you have a dataset of sales figures, Copilot might automatically identify a downward trend in sales for a particular month and offer suggestions on possible causes or actions.

- **Trend Analysis**: Copilot can generate charts and graphs that help you visually interpret trends and data patterns.

    o **Example**: If you have a large dataset of monthly sales, Copilot can suggest a line chart that shows sales performance over time, helping you visualize trends and spot irregularities.

2. Formula Suggestions and Generation

- **Formula Assistance**: Copilot can generate complex formulas for you, suggesting the most appropriate ones based on the context of your data.

    o **Example**: If you want to calculate the average of a range of cells, Copilot can automatically insert the formula for AVERAGE, or it can suggest a more complex formula, such as IF or VLOOKUP, based on the data you're working with.

- **Dynamic Formula Recommendations**: Copilot can recommend formulas and functions based on your specific needs, whether it's for calculating averages, summing data, or looking up values across multiple datasets.

    o **Example**: If you're working with financial data and need to calculate a return on investment (ROI), Copilot could automatically suggest the ROI = (Gain - Cost) / Cost formula and help you apply it.

3. Data Cleansing and Preparation

- **Data Cleaning**: Copilot can help clean up messy datasets by suggesting ways to remove duplicates, handle missing values, or standardize data formats.

  - **Example**: If you have a column of names with inconsistent formatting (e.g., some in uppercase, some in lowercase), Copilot might suggest a PROPER function to standardize the names to title case.

- **Missing Data Handling**: Copilot can identify missing or incomplete data and suggest ways to fill in gaps or remove incomplete entries.

  - **Example**: If a dataset has missing values, Copilot can recommend using an average or median value to fill those gaps, ensuring your analysis is not disrupted by incomplete data.

4. Automating Repetitive Tasks

- **Task Automation**: Copilot can automate repetitive tasks such as data entry, calculations, and formatting, saving you time on mundane tasks.

  - **Example**: If you're constantly entering sales data for each quarter, Copilot can create a template that automates the entry process based on previous data, reducing manual input.

- **Batch Processing**: If you have large datasets, Copilot can help with batch operations such as applying a formula to multiple columns or rows or adjusting formatting across the entire worksheet.

  - **Example**: Copilot could automatically apply conditional formatting to all rows based on sales performance, highlighting cells that meet specific criteria (e.g., sales above a certain threshold).

5. Data Visualization

- **Chart and Graph Recommendations**: Copilot can suggest the best charts or graphs based on your data to help visualize trends and insights clearly.

  - **Example**: If you're tracking monthly revenue and expenses, Copilot might recommend a bar chart or a line chart to visualize the comparison, ensuring that the data is represented in the most informative way.

- **Dynamic Visualization Creation**: Copilot can generate dynamic charts that automatically update as your data changes, providing you with real-time visual feedback on performance.

  - **Example**: If you're tracking a project timeline, Copilot might suggest a Gantt chart that automatically updates as you adjust the start or end dates of tasks.

6. Scenario Analysis and Forecasting

- **Scenario Analysis**: Copilot can help you model different business scenarios and suggest what-if analyses based on your data. This is useful for forecasting and making data-driven decisions.

- **Example**: If you have sales data and want to forecast future sales, Copilot could help model different scenarios based on historical data and suggest growth or decline projections.

- **Forecasting**: Copilot can use historical data to create forecasts for future performance, making it easier to plan and make informed decisions.

  - **Example**: If you're tracking monthly expenses and income, Copilot can predict future expenses or revenue based on past trends.

7. Collaboration and Real-Time Feedback

- **Real-Time Suggestions**: When collaborating with others in Excel, Copilot can provide real-time feedback, suggest edits, or highlight potential issues.

  - **Example**: If you're working on a financial model with a colleague, Copilot might suggest optimizing certain assumptions or improving data accuracy, making the collaboration more effective.

- **Commenting and Review**: Copilot can help with the review process by automatically generating comments for specific parts of the document or suggesting revisions to ensure the data is accurate and meaningful.

  - **Example**: If you are preparing a financial analysis, Copilot might add comments to explain calculations or suggest areas where data could be missing or incorrect.

8. Natural Language Queries

- **Natural Language Processing**: Copilot allows you to interact with your data in a conversational way. You can ask questions in natural language, and Copilot will process the query and return insights or perform actions accordingly.

  - **Example**: You can type or ask, "What were the total sales for Q2?" and Copilot will instantly provide the correct sum from your data, saving time on complex queries.

- **Custom Reports via Natural Language**: You can create custom reports by simply asking Copilot to generate a specific view of the data based on your needs.

  - **Example**: If you need to see a summary of customer purchases by region, you can ask, "Show me a summary of customer purchases by region," and Copilot will generate a pivot table or chart to match your request.

9. Data Security and Compliance

- **Data Protection**: Copilot can provide suggestions to enhance data security and ensure that your work complies with privacy standards. It can help you identify sensitive information in your spreadsheets, such as personally identifiable information (PII), and suggest appropriate actions.

  - **Example**: If your Excel sheet contains customer contact information, Copilot might alert you to ensure proper encryption and access controls are in place.

- **Audit and Compliance Checks**: Copilot can run checks on your data for compliance with standards or regulations, such as GDPR, and suggest actions to address any compliance gaps.

o **Example**: Copilot can highlight any data that may be sensitive and recommend anonymizing or removing that data to meet compliance requirements.

10. Customizable Dashboards

- **Dashboard Creation**: Copilot can help you create customized dashboards to display important metrics, KPIs, and other data points, making it easier to track performance.

  o **Example**: If you're tracking a project's progress, Copilot can suggest a dashboard layout with key metrics like completed tasks, deadlines, and project costs, automatically pulling data from your spreadsheet.

How to Leverage Microsoft Excel with Copilot:

1. **Ask Questions in Natural Language**: Save time by using natural language queries to retrieve specific information or perform calculations instead of manually setting up complex formulas.

2. **Automate Repetitive Tasks**: Use Copilot to automate routine tasks like data entry, formatting, and calculations, freeing up time for more strategic work.

3. **Visualize Your Data**: Leverage Copilot's suggestions for charts, graphs, and other visual elements that make your data easier to understand and present to others.

4. **Collaborate More Effectively**: Utilize Copilot's real-time suggestions and feedback during collaborative efforts, ensuring that the data is accurate and up-to-date.

5. **Ensure Data Quality**: Let Copilot help clean and organize your data, ensuring that your analysis is based on accurate and consistent information.

Microsoft Excel with **Copilot** integration significantly enhances the tool's ability to perform data analysis, automate tasks, provide insights, and improve collaboration, all while saving time and increasing productivity. Whether you're analyzing data, creating financial models, or preparing reports, Copilot helps you work smarter and more efficiently.

Microsoft PowerPoint

Microsoft PowerPoint, as part of the **Microsoft 365** suite, is a powerful tool for creating presentations. With the integration of **Microsoft Copilot**, PowerPoint becomes even more intelligent and efficient, providing AI-powered assistance to create, design, and refine presentations effortlessly.

Here's how **Microsoft Copilot** can enhance your PowerPoint experience:

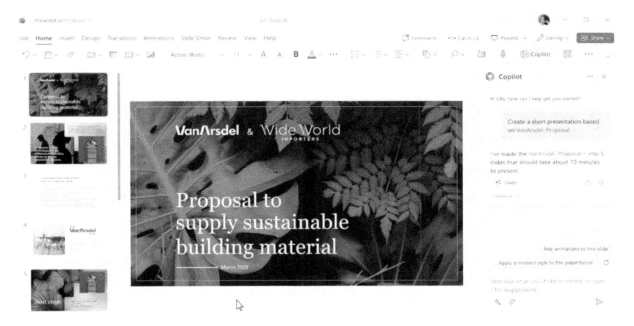

1. Content Creation and Slide Generation

- **Automated Slide Creation**: Copilot can help generate slides based on a topic or content you provide. It can create slides with appropriate titles, text, bullet points, and even suggest accompanying visuals based on the content.

  - **Example**: If you provide a brief or a few sentences about a topic like "The Impact of Artificial Intelligence in Healthcare," Copilot can generate a presentation outline and create slides with relevant content, including key points on the topic.

- **Text Summarization**: Copilot can automatically summarize long pieces of text or documents and convert them into concise bullet points or slide content.

  - **Example**: If you upload a lengthy report, Copilot can break down the key points and transform them into digestible bullet points for your presentation.

2. Design and Layout Suggestions

- **Smart Design Suggestions**: Copilot can recommend design themes, layouts, and color schemes based on your content and purpose. It helps ensure that your slides are visually appealing and professional.

  - **Example**: If you're creating a business presentation, Copilot might suggest a clean, corporate design with complementary colors and fonts that align with your company's branding.

- **Slide Formatting**: Copilot can format your slides, ensuring they are properly aligned, balanced, and consistent throughout the presentation.

  - **Example**: Copilot can adjust the placement of text boxes and images to ensure that the layout looks balanced and clean, making sure the slides don't appear overcrowded.

3. Multimedia and Visual Content

- **Image and Media Suggestions**: Copilot can recommend images, videos, and other multimedia elements to enhance your slides, based on the context of the presentation.

  - **Example**: If you're presenting on climate change, Copilot might suggest relevant images of natural disasters, infographics, or video clips that align with your topic.

- **Charts and Graphs**: Copilot can suggest appropriate charts and graphs to visually represent data, ensuring that complex information is easy to understand.

  - **Example**: If you're presenting sales data, Copilot can recommend bar charts, pie charts, or line graphs to help your audience better visualize trends and comparisons.

4. Content Optimization

- **Tone and Style Adjustments**: Copilot can help adjust the tone of your presentation, ensuring it matches the intended audience. Whether you're presenting to executives, peers, or a classroom, Copilot can make sure your language is appropriate.

  - **Example**: If you're presenting to a group of executives, Copilot might suggest more formal language, while for a classroom audience, it may recommend a simpler, more engaging tone.

- **Content Clarity and Brevity**: Copilot can help refine your slides by suggesting more concise wording or adjusting phrasing to make your content clearer and more impactful.

  - **Example**: If a slide contains long paragraphs, Copilot might recommend shortening them into short, punchy bullet points for easier readability.

5. AI-Powered Speaker Notes

- **Automatic Speaker Notes**: Copilot can generate speaker notes to accompany your slides, providing you with prompts, talking points, and key points to emphasize during your presentation.

  - **Example**: If you create a slide about "The Benefits of AI in Education," Copilot might provide notes such as, "Explain how AI helps personalize learning experiences and improve engagement."

- **Personalized Script Suggestions**: Copilot can suggest personalized scripts for specific slides, making your delivery smoother and more confident.

  - **Example**: If you need to explain a complex chart, Copilot can suggest a simple script to help break down the data and explain it effectively.

6. Real-Time Collaboration and Feedback

- **Real-Time Suggestions**: Copilot offers real-time feedback while you're building the presentation, suggesting improvements, adding content, or even recommending visual enhancements.

  - **Example**: If you're presenting data, Copilot might suggest adding a summary of key points or offering a call to action at the end of the presentation to ensure clarity.

- **Collaborative Review**: Copilot can help you work with collaborators by analyzing their feedback and automatically adjusting the presentation accordingly. It can also help identify areas that need further input or clarification.

  - **Example**: If you're working with a team, Copilot can automatically incorporate comments, revisions, and suggestions into the slides, ensuring the final version reflects everyone's input.

7. Natural Language Commands

- **Voice or Text Commands for Slide Management**: Copilot allows you to control your presentation through natural language commands. You can ask Copilot to add, move, or remove slides, or even change the layout.

  - **Example**: You can say, "Add a slide after this one with the title 'Conclusion'" or "Change the layout of the third slide to a comparison layout," and Copilot will make those adjustments for you.

- **Content Search and Insertion**: Copilot can help you quickly find and insert content, such as images, charts, or text from other documents.

  - **Example**: If you need to reference a specific figure from an Excel sheet, you can ask, "Insert the data from the sales table," and Copilot will automatically insert the relevant data into your presentation.

8. Real-Time Presentation Support

- **On-the-Fly Adjustments**: During your presentation, Copilot can offer real-time suggestions, such as reminding you of key points to discuss or helping you adjust the pacing.

  - **Example**: If you're running out of time, Copilot can suggest skipping certain slides or summarizing the content more quickly to stay on track.

- **Audience Engagement**: Copilot can suggest ways to engage your audience, such as posing questions, creating polls, or adding interactive elements to your presentation.

  - **Example**: If you're presenting to a group of students, Copilot might suggest adding a quick poll or interactive Q&A session to encourage participation.

9. Presentation Refinement

- **Speech Coaching**: Copilot can assist in speech delivery by providing tips on pacing, tone, and emphasis during your presentation. It can even analyze your slide content and suggest ways to deliver it more effectively.

  - **Example**: If you have a particularly data-heavy slide, Copilot might suggest slowing down and explaining key trends more clearly, ensuring the audience grasps the information.

- **Visual Consistency**: Copilot ensures that all your slides are visually consistent, with proper alignment, font usage, and color schemes. It can automatically apply consistent design principles across all slides.

o **Example**: If you use different fonts or colors across slides, Copilot can suggest using a uniform font and color palette to maintain a professional appearance.

10. Custom Templates and Branding

- **Template Recommendations**: Copilot can suggest custom templates based on the purpose of your presentation, such as business presentations, academic reports, or sales pitches.

  o **Example**: If you're preparing a product launch presentation, Copilot may suggest a dynamic, visually appealing template that aligns with your brand's style guide.

- **Brand Consistency**: If you upload your company's branding guidelines or templates, Copilot will ensure all your slides follow the approved fonts, colors, and logo placement, keeping your presentation on-brand.

  o **Example**: If your company uses a specific set of colors for all presentations, Copilot will automatically apply these colors to the design of the slides.

11. Export and Sharing Assistance

- **Exporting to Other Formats**: Copilot can help you export your PowerPoint presentation to other formats, such as PDF, video, or even an interactive format suitable for online sharing.

  o **Example**: If you need to export your presentation as a PDF for printing, Copilot can handle the conversion, ensuring the layout is preserved.

- **Sharing and Collaboration**: Copilot assists with sharing the presentation with others and managing collaboration settings, such as allowing others to edit or comment.

  o **Example**: If you're presenting to a team, Copilot can help share the presentation with the group, enabling real-time collaboration.

How to Leverage Microsoft PowerPoint with Copilot:

1. **Start with an Outline**: Provide Copilot with an outline or topic, and let it generate the slides for you, saving time on content creation.

2. **Use Smart Design Features**: Let Copilot recommend professional design layouts, color schemes, and fonts to ensure a polished presentation.

3. **Refine and Optimize Content**: Use Copilot's suggestions to refine your slides, make the content more concise, and ensure clarity and impact.

4. **Collaborate Effectively**: Take advantage of Copilot's real-time collaboration features, integrating feedback and suggestions seamlessly.

5. **Practice Your Delivery**: Use Copilot's speech coaching and slide tips to ensure a confident and engaging delivery during your presentation.

Microsoft PowerPoint with **Copilot** integration significantly improves the process of creating, refining, and delivering presentations. With AI-driven insights, automatic suggestions, and design recommendations, it makes presentations more effective, professional, and engaging, all while saving time and enhancing collaboration.

Microsoft Outlook

Microsoft Outlook, as part of the **Microsoft 365** suite, is a leading email and calendar management application. When integrated with **Microsoft Copilot**, Outlook becomes even more powerful, offering AI-driven features that enhance productivity, organization, and communication.

Here's how **Microsoft Copilot** can improve your **Microsoft Outlook** experience in 2025:

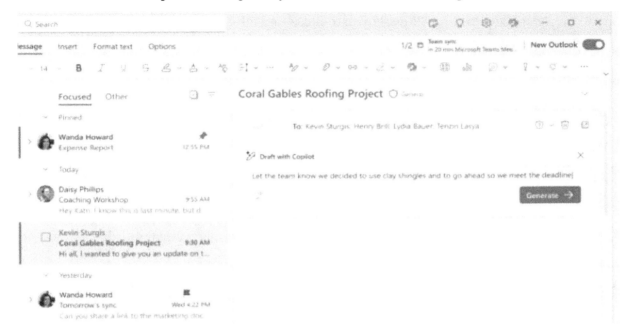

1. Email Composition and Management

- **AI-Powered Email Drafting**: Copilot can help you write emails by suggesting professional language, rephrasing sentences for clarity, or even drafting complete responses based on your brief input.

    o **Example**: If you start composing an email, Copilot might suggest an appropriate subject line or offer responses for common phrases like "Thank you for your email" or "I look forward to hearing from you."

- **Smart Email Summarization**: Copilot can scan long email threads and summarize them, extracting the key points for you to quickly catch up without reading everything.

    o **Example**: If you're in an email chain with multiple participants and a lot of back-and-forth, Copilot might summarize the conversation, focusing on the most important updates and action items.

- **Reply Suggestions**: Copilot can suggest quick replies based on the content of the email you're reading. It can automatically draft short, polite responses like "Thank you" or "Noted."

    o **Example**: When you receive an email with simple requests like meeting dates or confirmation, Copilot might suggest "Confirming the meeting for Thursday" as a reply.

2. Inbox Organization and Prioritization

- **Smart Inbox Sorting**: Copilot can intelligently sort and prioritize emails based on their importance. It can highlight urgent emails, emails from specific contacts, or emails that require immediate attention.

  - **Example**: Copilot might categorize your emails into priority groups: Important, Urgent, and Low Priority, allowing you to focus on high-priority tasks first.

- **Automatic Folder Organization**: Copilot can automatically organize incoming emails into designated folders, based on the sender or subject matter. This keeps your inbox tidy and more manageable.

  - **Example**: If you receive regular newsletters, Copilot might automatically move them to a "Newsletters" folder to keep your inbox focused on work-related emails.

- **Email Cleanup**: Copilot can help clean up your inbox by suggesting old or less important emails to delete, archive, or unsubscribe from, freeing up space and reducing clutter.

  - **Example**: Copilot could recommend deleting outdated emails or unsubscribing from newsletters you no longer read, helping keep your inbox streamlined.

3. Calendar Management and Scheduling

- **Smart Scheduling**: Copilot can help schedule meetings and appointments by suggesting available time slots based on your calendar and the recipient's availability.

  - **Example**: If you're trying to schedule a meeting with someone, Copilot can analyze both your calendar and theirs, suggesting open time slots that work for both parties.

- **Meeting Preparation**: Copilot can assist with preparing for meetings by suggesting agenda items, creating reminders, or pulling in relevant documents from your emails or OneDrive.

  - **Example**: If you have an upcoming meeting with a client, Copilot can gather previous email exchanges with that client and suggest talking points for the meeting.

- **AI-Powered Reminders**: Copilot can automatically create reminders for upcoming meetings, deadlines, and tasks, and ensure you stay on top of important events.

  - **Example**: Copilot can automatically remind you about a meeting 30 minutes before it starts and alert you to any preparations you need to make.

4. AI-Powered Task Management

- **Task Generation**: Copilot can generate tasks from emails, calendar events, and meetings, helping you manage your to-do list more effectively.

  - **Example**: If you receive an email with a request to "send the report by tomorrow," Copilot can automatically create a task in your To-Do list with a reminder.

- **Task Prioritization**: Copilot can help you prioritize tasks based on deadlines, importance, and urgency, ensuring you tackle the most critical items first.

  - **Example**: If multiple tasks are due soon, Copilot might highlight the ones that are time-sensitive, while suggesting that others be deferred or rescheduled.

5. Meeting Insights and Follow-ups

- **Post-Meeting Summaries**: Copilot can generate summaries after meetings based on the calendar event, notes, and email threads, providing you with a quick recap of what was discussed.

  - **Example**: After a meeting, Copilot might generate a summary of key action items and decisions made, which can be shared with participants.

- **Follow-Up Reminders**: Copilot can remind you to follow up on tasks or emails after a meeting, ensuring that action items are not forgotten.

  - **Example**: If you promised to send an email after a meeting, Copilot can create a reminder or draft the follow-up email for you.

6. Enhanced Search and Email Retrieval

- **Contextual Search**: Copilot enhances the Outlook search experience by allowing you to find relevant emails, meetings, or attachments based on natural language queries.

  - **Example**: You can type "Find the email about the marketing meeting from last Thursday," and Copilot will quickly retrieve the relevant conversation.

- **Advanced Filtering**: Copilot can help you filter your inbox by specific criteria such as sender, keywords, or attachments, making it easier to find the emails you need.

  - **Example**: If you're looking for an email with an attachment from a particular sender, Copilot can filter emails by these criteria.

7. Attachment Management

- **Smart Attachment Suggestions**: Copilot can suggest attaching relevant files based on the content of your email or previous communications.

  - **Example**: If you're drafting an email about a report, Copilot might suggest attaching the most recent version of the report, based on previous email exchanges.

- **Attachment Organization**: Copilot can help you organize attachments from your emails by automatically saving them to OneDrive or your preferred storage location.

  - **Example**: If you receive multiple attachments over a period, Copilot could organize them into folders based on their type or subject matter for easy access.

8. Security and Privacy Enhancements

- **Privacy Alerts**: Copilot can alert you to any potential security or privacy risks in your email communications, such as sharing sensitive data or attachments with unauthorized recipients.

  - **Example**: If you accidentally send an email to a wrong recipient, Copilot can alert you to this issue and prompt you to retract the message if needed.

- **Phishing Detection**: Copilot can analyze emails for phishing attempts or suspicious links and warn you if an email seems suspicious.

- **Example**: If you receive an email that looks like a phishing attempt, Copilot might warn you, helping you avoid potential security breaches.

9. Email Personalization and Branding

- **Signature Personalization**: Copilot can help you personalize your email signature by suggesting text, graphics, or contact information based on your role or preferences.

  - **Example**: If you're working on a corporate email, Copilot might suggest adding your company logo or using a specific signature format.

- **Consistent Email Tone**: Copilot can help you maintain a consistent tone in your email communications, whether professional, friendly, or casual, depending on your preferences.

  - **Example**: If you send a message to a colleague, Copilot might suggest a more informal tone, while for external clients, it might recommend a more formal, professional approach.

10. Real-Time Collaboration and Communication

- **Collaborative Emails**: Copilot can assist you with drafting emails when collaborating on projects, making it easier to communicate with teams or clients in a professional and concise manner.

  - **Example**: If you're working with a team on a project, Copilot might suggest phrases for team coordination, progress updates, or specific tasks.

- **Task Delegation**: Copilot can help delegate tasks directly within emails, turning requests or assignments into actionable items with reminders and due dates.

  - **Example**: If you assign tasks to colleagues via email, Copilot can automatically set reminders or add the tasks to your project management tool.

How to Leverage Microsoft Outlook with Copilot:

1. **Compose and Respond Efficiently**: Use Copilot to draft emails or reply to common inquiries, speeding up communication while maintaining professionalism.

2. **Stay Organized**: Let Copilot help sort and prioritize your inbox, ensuring that important messages don't get lost in the noise.

3. **Manage Your Calendar**: Use Copilot to schedule meetings and ensure that your calendar is always up-to-date with minimal effort.

4. **Create Tasks and Follow-Ups**: Let Copilot generate tasks and reminders from your emails, meetings, and deadlines, ensuring nothing falls through the cracks.

5. **Optimize Search**: Use natural language queries to quickly find relevant emails, attachments, or meetings.

6. **Collaborate Seamlessly**: Leverage Copilot's suggestions for efficient team communication and collaboration via email.

With Microsoft Outlook and Copilot integration, managing emails, scheduling meetings, and staying organized becomes more efficient and intelligent.

Copilot's AI capabilities ensure that your communication is streamlined, your productivity is enhanced, and your workflow is optimized. Whether you're composing emails, organizing your inbox, or managing meetings, Copilot can help you work smarter and faster.

CHAPTER FIVE
ADVANCED FUNCTIONALITIES

Customizing Copilot's Suggestions

Customizing **Microsoft Copilot's** suggestions in **Microsoft Outlook** (and other Microsoft 365 applications) allows you to tailor the AI to match your specific needs, preferences, and workflows. By doing so, you can ensure that Copilot's insights and recommendations align with your communication style, priorities, and professional requirements. Here's how you can customize **Copilot's suggestions** for a more personalized and effective experience:

1. Setting Up Personalized Preferences

- **Tone and Style**: You can adjust Copilot to generate responses in the tone and style you prefer, whether formal, friendly, concise, or detailed. For instance, if you primarily deal with professional clients, you can set a more formal communication style.

    - **How to Customize**: In the Outlook settings, go to the **"AI settings"** or **"Copilot preferences"**, and select your desired tone for emails. You can choose between options like "Professional," "Casual," or even "Friendly."

2. Keyword and Topic Preferences

- **Context-Based Suggestions**: Copilot can be customized to prioritize certain keywords or topics that are important to your work. For example, if you're frequently discussing project timelines, Copilot can offer suggestions related to project management terms or deadlines.

    - **How to Customize**: Under the **"AI Preferences"** menu, you can list frequently used terms or keywords, or you can adjust your settings to focus on specific subject matter or industries.

3. Smart Reply Filters

- **Control the Suggestions for Quick Replies**: You can control the types of **quick reply suggestions** that Copilot offers. For instance, if you're often asked for confirmations or scheduling, Copilot can prioritize offering those types of responses.

    - **How to Customize**: In the Copilot settings, enable or disable specific types of suggestions, such as **"Confirmation responses"**, **"Scheduling suggestions"**, or **"Follow-up prompts."**

4. Integration with Your Contacts and Calendar

- **Tailored Calendar and Meeting Suggestions**: Copilot can give better meeting and scheduling suggestions by learning from your calendar history. It can offer meeting times based on your most frequent availability, and it can suggest meeting durations and locations.

    - **How to Customize**: Review and adjust **"Calendar preferences"** in the AI settings to ensure Copilot understands your most common work hours and preferred locations for meetings (such as virtual or in-person).

5. Content Sensitivity and Privacy

- **Sensitive Information Alerts**: Copilot can be customized to flag or avoid suggesting responses that include sensitive information, such as financial details, confidential company data, or personal matters.

    o **How to Customize**: Adjust the **"Privacy and Security Settings"** to help Copilot filter out suggestions that might compromise confidentiality, or restrict it from drafting emails with sensitive data.

6. Follow-Up and Reminder Customization

- **Set Follow-Up Preferences**: Copilot can remind you to follow up on certain emails or meetings, but you can adjust these reminders based on the priority or time frame.

    o **How to Customize**: In the settings, you can set the type of reminders you want—whether they're for **urgent** follow-ups (e.g., after a week) or for **low-priority** items (e.g., after a month).

7. Email Summarization Preferences

- **Customizing Email Summaries**: Copilot can generate summaries of long email threads. You can adjust how much detail is included in the summary (e.g., highlight action items only, or include full context).

    o **How to Customize**: Adjust **"Summary Depth"** in the Copilot preferences, selecting **brief summaries**, **detailed summaries**, or **action-item-focused summaries**.

8. Attachment Suggestions

- **Customized Attachment Handling**: Copilot can suggest files and attachments based on the context of the email, but you can adjust which types of files it should prioritize.

    o **How to Customize**: In the **"Attachment Settings"**, you can specify which types of files (documents, images, PDFs, etc.) should be considered for suggestion. You can also configure it to exclude certain folders or file types that aren't relevant.

9. Language and Region Preferences

- **Localized Suggestions**: If you work across multiple regions or languages, Copilot can be tailored to offer region-specific suggestions, such as date formats, currencies, or region-specific phrasings.

    o **How to Customize**: Go to **"Language Settings"** in the Copilot preferences and specify your primary language and regional settings to adjust language-specific suggestions.

10. Behavioral Learning Over Time

- **Adaptive Learning**: Copilot can adapt its suggestions based on your behavior. For example, if you consistently ignore specific suggestions or prefer a different approach, Copilot will learn and adjust over time.

o **How to Customize**: In your **"Learning Settings"**, you can choose whether you want Copilot to learn from your actions or stick to default behaviors. You can also delete or reset Copilot's learning data to start fresh.

11. Predefined Templates for Frequent Tasks

- **Custom Templates**: For tasks that you do frequently—such as follow-up emails, meeting requests, or project status updates—Copilot can suggest using predefined templates. These templates can be created according to your style and needs.

  o **How to Customize**: Under **"Template Management"**, you can create and save templates for common email types. Copilot can then suggest these templates when appropriate, saving you time on repetitive tasks.

12. Task-Related Suggestions

- **Task and Action Item Prioritization**: Copilot can suggest tasks based on the content of your emails. For instance, if you receive an email with an action item, Copilot might suggest creating a task for it. You can specify how these tasks should be categorized or prioritized.

  o **How to Customize**: Go to **"Task Preferences"**, where you can define whether Copilot should create tasks for you automatically and what type of tasks to prioritize (e.g., urgent vs. non-urgent).

13. Feedback Loop for Improving Suggestions

- **Providing Feedback on Suggestions**: If Copilot suggests something you don't like or doesn't quite fit your needs, you can provide feedback to improve its future suggestions. This helps refine Copilot's suggestions over time.

  o **How to Customize**: In the settings, look for a **"Feedback"** option where you can rate Copilot's suggestions (e.g., thumbs up or thumbs down) and give specific feedback on how to improve future recommendations.

By customizing **Microsoft Copilot's suggestions**, you can create a more efficient and personalized experience, ensuring that the AI assists you exactly how you need it. Whether you're composing emails, scheduling meetings, or managing tasks, taking advantage of these settings will ensure that Copilot fits.

Integrating Third-Party Applications

Integrating third-party applications with **Microsoft Copilot** can significantly expand its functionality, allowing you to streamline your workflow, manage projects, and interact with various tools directly within the Microsoft 365 environment. Here's a guide on how to integrate third-party applications with **Microsoft Copilot** in 2025, enhancing productivity and boosting the power of your digital ecosystem.

1. Why Integrate Third-Party Applications with Copilot?

- **Increased Productivity**: By connecting your favourite third-party apps (like project management tools, CRM systems, or data analytics platforms), you can automate tasks, reduce manual input, and enhance collaboration.

- **Data Consolidation**: Integrating apps allows Copilot to access data from multiple sources, improving its suggestions, insights, and task recommendations.

- **Streamlined Communication**: Third-party integrations can help keep communication consistent across various platforms without needing to switch between apps, saving you time and effort.

2. Types of Third-Party Applications You Can Integrate

- **Productivity & Project Management Tools**: Apps like **Trello, Asana, Monday.com**, or **Jira** can be connected to Copilot to automatically create tasks, manage projects, and provide updates.

- **Customer Relationship Management (CRM)**: Tools like **Salesforce, HubSpot**, or **Zoho CRM** can be integrated to manage contacts, track leads, and automate email communications directly within Outlook or other Microsoft 365 apps.

- **Finance & Accounting Software**: Integrating financial tools like **QuickBooks, Xero**, or **FreshBooks** allows Copilot to assist in tracking expenses, generating invoices, and managing financial reports.

- **Cloud Storage & File Sharing**: Services like **Google Drive, Dropbox**, or **Box** can be connected to easily share and manage files, ensuring seamless access across apps.

- **Communication Platforms**: Integrate messaging services like **Slack, Teams**, or **Zoom** for streamlined communication and video conferencing capabilities directly within your Microsoft 365 environment.

- **Marketing & Analytics Tools**: Integrating platforms such as **Mailchimp, Google Analytics**, or **Hootsuite** will enable Copilot to provide actionable insights, track campaigns, and manage social media updates.

3. Steps to Integrate Third-Party Applications with Copilot

To integrate third-party apps with **Microsoft Copilot**, you can follow these general steps (Note: Actual steps may vary depending on the application):

Step 1: Ensure Access to Microsoft 365 and Copilot

- Make sure your **Microsoft 365** subscription includes access to **Copilot**.

- Confirm that the third-party app you want to integrate is compatible with **Microsoft 365** and **Copilot**.

Step 2: Visit the Microsoft Store or App Marketplace

- Go to the **Microsoft AppSource** or **Microsoft Store** where apps that work with Microsoft 365 are listed.

- Search for the third-party application you want to integrate (e.g., **Trello, Salesforce**).

- Click on the app and follow the installation instructions to add it to your Microsoft 365 environment.

Step 3: Connect the App to Microsoft 365

- Once the app is installed, open the third-party app, and you will typically see an option to **connect** or **link** it to your Microsoft 365 account. You may need to log in using your Microsoft credentials.

- This process typically involves providing permissions for the third-party app to access your Microsoft 365 apps (such as Outlook, Teams, or SharePoint).

Step 4: Enable Copilot Integration

- Some third-party apps come with built-in integration for **Copilot**. If the app supports Copilot, you will need to enable it within the third-party application settings.

- For example, if you've integrated **Salesforce**, you can enable features that allow Copilot to pull customer data into Outlook or suggest sales strategies based on customer interactions.

Step 5: Customize Copilot's Workflow

- After integration, access Copilot's settings to tailor how it interacts with your third-party apps. You can adjust how often Copilot fetches data, the level of detail included in its suggestions, and how tasks from third-party apps are synced.

- For instance, if you've connected **Asana**, you might want Copilot to automatically generate tasks in Outlook when a new project milestone is added in **Asana**.

Step 6: Test the Integration

- Run a few tests to ensure the integration is functioning correctly. For instance, create a task in **Trello** and see if Copilot suggests the task in **Outlook** or automatically generates reminders.

- You can also test communication features. For example, if **Slack** is integrated, check if you can send messages from Outlook directly to **Slack** channels.

4. Customizing Integration with Microsoft Copilot

After integrating third-party apps with **Copilot**, here are some customizations you can make to get the most out of the integration:

Automated Task Creation and Notifications

- **Automate Task Management**: If you integrate project management tools like **Trello** or **Asana**, you can set Copilot to automatically create tasks based on emails, calendar events, or new project milestones.

  - Example: If you receive an email from a client with a deadline mentioned, Copilot can automatically create a task in **Trello** or **Microsoft To-Do** with the due date.

- **Set Task Reminders**: With tools like **Jira** or **Trello**, Copilot can send reminders about upcoming project deadlines directly within your Outlook.

Content Syncing and File Sharing

- If you've connected cloud storage apps like **Google Drive** or **OneDrive**, Copilot can automatically suggest relevant files for attachment when composing emails or working on documents.

  - Example: Copilot can recommend attaching the most recent project proposal from **Google Drive** when drafting an email about a project update.

Calendar Integration

- By connecting **Outlook** with third-party scheduling tools like **Calendly** or **Zoom**, Copilot can automatically propose meeting times, send calendar invites, and sync meetings across platforms.

  - Example: If you schedule a meeting in **Zoom**, Copilot can create the event in your **Outlook** calendar and suggest a follow-up email or to-do item.

Customer Insights and CRM Integration

- If your CRM system (like **Salesforce** or **HubSpot**) is integrated, Copilot can suggest email responses, remind you about sales leads, or pull customer data into your email drafts.

  - Example: When composing an email, Copilot can suggest inserting personalized content based on a customer's profile, recent activities, or product preferences from your CRM.

Marketing Insights

- For marketing tools like **Mailchimp** or **Google Analytics**, Copilot can suggest marketing-related tasks, like creating new email campaigns or reviewing social media performance.

  - Example: If Copilot notices a drop in website traffic (via **Google Analytics**), it can suggest drafting an email or creating a report about potential reasons and solutions.

5. Popular Third-Party App Integrations with Copilot

- **Salesforce**: Manage customer relationships, track leads, and automate follow-up actions within **Outlook**.

- **Slack**: Send messages and collaborate seamlessly across both platforms.

- **Trello/Asana**: Manage tasks and projects directly within Microsoft 365 apps.

- **Zoom/Teams**: Schedule, join, and manage video meetings directly from Outlook or Teams.

- **Google Analytics/Mailchimp**: Use Copilot to pull in marketing data and suggest campaign improvements.

6. Troubleshooting Integration Issues

- **Ensure Compatibility**: Verify that the third-party app is compatible with **Microsoft Copilot** and Microsoft 365.

- **Check Permissions**: Make sure you've granted necessary permissions for data sharing between Microsoft 365 and the third-party app.

- **Update Software**: Both **Microsoft 365** and third-party apps should be updated to ensure smooth integration.

- **Contact Support**: If integration fails, contact support for either Microsoft or the third-party app for troubleshooting guidance.

Integrating third-party applications with **Microsoft Copilot** creates a seamless, efficient workflow, allowing you to access a broader range of tools and data while maintaining productivity within your Microsoft 365 environment. Customizing these integrations based on your needs enhances Copilot's utility and ensures that it fits perfectly into your everyday tasks and business processes.

Utilizing Copilot's API for Developers

Utilizing Microsoft Copilot's API for Developers allows developers to enhance their applications, services, or workflows by leveraging the powerful AI features of Copilot within their custom solutions. With Copilot's API, you can integrate natural language processing, task automation, real-time assistance, and more, directly into your applications, creating a seamless experience for users.

Here's a step-by-step guide for developers on how to utilize **Copilot's API** in 2025:

1. Accessing Microsoft Copilot's API

Before integrating Microsoft Copilot's capabilities into your application, you need to access the API.

- **Microsoft Graph API**: Copilot's API is generally available through **Microsoft Graph**—a unified endpoint that allows developers to interact with data across Microsoft 365 apps and services. Microsoft Graph provides access to various Copilot features, such as analyzing documents, handling calendar events, and more.

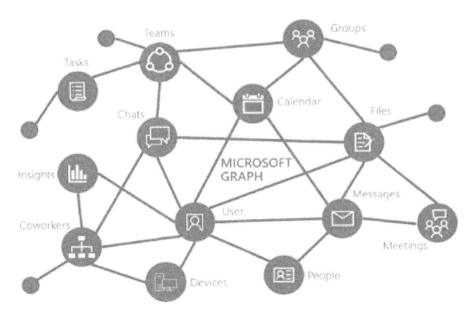

- **Microsoft Azure OpenAI Service**: For more advanced AI features, developers can also use the **Azure OpenAI Service**, which provides access to GPT-powered models, including those that power **Copilot**.

Steps to Get Started with API Access:

1. **Create an Azure account**: Sign up for **Azure** if you don't have one already.

2. **Subscribe to the OpenAI Service**: From your Azure portal, subscribe to the **OpenAI service** to get access to Copilot's language models.

3. **Create a new project**: Once you've subscribed, create a new project and obtain an API key for accessing the services.

2. Integrating Copilot's Capabilities via API

Once you have access to the API, you can integrate Copilot's capabilities into your application using the following methods:

a. Natural Language Processing (NLP) for Task Automation

Use Copilot's **NLP capabilities** to enable your application to interpret natural language queries or instructions and respond accordingly.

- **Example**: You could integrate the API to allow users to write emails or documents in natural language and let the AI generate drafts or suggestions.

- **Request Example** (using OpenAI API for text generation):

json

CopyEdit

```json
{
  "model": "gpt-4",
  "prompt": "Write a professional email confirming the meeting at 3 PM tomorrow.",
  "temperature": 0.7,
  "max_tokens": 150
}
```

- **Response Example**:

json

CopyEdit

```json
{
  "text": "Dear [Recipient],\n\nI am writing to confirm our meeting scheduled for 3 PM tomorrow. Please let me know if there are any changes to the timing.\n\nBest regards,\n[Your Name]"
}
```

b. Automating Tasks in Microsoft 365

The **Microsoft Graph API** enables the automation of tasks within Microsoft 365 services like **Outlook**, **Teams**, and **SharePoint**. Developers can build custom workflows to automatically create meetings, schedule events, or update documents based on natural language input.

- **Example**: Automating meeting scheduling via Copilot in Outlook.
- **Request Example** (using Microsoft Graph API to create an event):

json

CopyEdit

```json
{
  "subject": "Team Meeting",
  "start": {
    "dateTime": "2025-03-15T09:00:00",
    "timeZone": "UTC"
  },
  "end": {
    "dateTime": "2025-03-15T10:00:00",
    "timeZone": "UTC"
  },
```

```
  "attendees": [

    {

      "emailAddress": {

        "address": "user@example.com",

        "name": "John Doe"

      },

      "type": "required"

    }

  ]

}
```

- **Response Example**: Confirmation that the meeting is scheduled successfully in the calendar.

c. Document Understanding and Editing

Copilot can be used to analyze and edit documents through **Microsoft Word** and **OneDrive** integrations.

- **Example**: Integrating Copilot to edit or summarize text in Word.
- **Request Example** (using OpenAI API to summarize text):

json

CopyEdit

```
{

  "model": "gpt-4",

  "prompt": "Summarize the following text for a presentation: [Insert text here]",

  "temperature": 0.6,

  "max_tokens": 100

}
```

- **Response Example**:

json

CopyEdit

```
{

  "text": "This document highlights the key findings of our recent research on [Topic]. It covers the methodology, results, and conclusions with a focus on [specific detail]."
```

}

3. Utilizing Copilot's API for Custom Solutions

The power of **Copilot's API** lies in its ability to customize workflows, data processing, and natural language tasks. Developers can build custom solutions tailored to specific industries or workflows, such as:

a. Integrating Copilot with Customer Relationship Management (CRM) Systems

- **Example**: Automatically sending follow-up emails to clients based on meeting notes or customer data stored in the CRM.

- **Request Example**: Integrate with **Salesforce** or **HubSpot** to send automated follow-up emails after a sales call.

- **API Call**: Integrate customer details, meeting schedules, and AI-generated responses using the API for follow-ups.

b. Creating Custom Chatbots for Your Business

- **Example**: Develop a chatbot that can assist customers with inquiries based on your company's FAQ and real-time support data.

- **Request Example**: Using **Microsoft Bot Framework** alongside Copilot's NLP capabilities to generate responses to customer queries in natural language.

- **Integration with Bot Framework**:

  o Create a bot that pulls from **Copilot** to generate conversational replies.

  o Use Microsoft's Bot Framework SDK to link Copilot's natural language capabilities with a bot deployed on **Microsoft Teams** or your website.

4. Customizing Copilot's Responses and Behavior

Developers can fine-tune Copilot's behavior to better suit their application's needs:

a. Set Parameters for Tone and Formality

- Developers can specify the tone of responses from Copilot (e.g., professional, casual, or humorous) through API parameters.

- **Request Example**: Specify the tone of an email or message.

json

CopyEdit

```
{
  "model": "gpt-4",
  "prompt": "Write a professional email thanking a client for a partnership. Tone: Formal.",
  "temperature": 0.5,
```

```
"max_tokens": 150
}
```

b. Incorporate Context-Aware Suggestions

- Developers can feed Copilot with additional context, such as the user's previous interactions or preferences, to help it make more relevant suggestions or automate more complex workflows.

- **Example**: After integrating Copilot with a project management tool, Copilot can suggest tasks based on a project's status or historical data.

- **API Call**: Provide context through request parameters (e.g., project status, task type, etc.) for a more personalized response.

5. Handling Errors and Troubleshooting API Issues

- **API Rate Limits**: Microsoft Copilot's API may have rate limits depending on your subscription plan. Be sure to check the limits to avoid hitting the maximum requests per minute or day.

- **Error Handling**: Implement error handling in your code to manage API issues like timeouts or invalid API keys.

json

CopyEdit

```json
{
  "error": {
    "code": "Unauthorized",
    "message": "The request is missing an API key or the key is invalid."
  }
}
```

- **Best Practices**: Implement retry mechanisms, optimize requests, and monitor the API usage regularly to ensure smooth integration.

6. Example Use Cases for Developers

- **Customer Support Automation**: Automatically generate support tickets, categorize issues, and provide responses based on customer queries using Copilot's NLP capabilities.

- **Smart Assistant Applications**: Build custom assistants that can understand user input and interact with a variety of systems like emails, calendars, and task management apps.

- **Document Management Solutions**: Automate document creation, summarization, and editing in tools like **Microsoft Word** and **Excel**.

7. Security and Data Privacy Considerations

When integrating third-party applications or handling sensitive user data via Copilot's API, be sure to:

- Implement secure authentication methods like OAuth or API tokens.

- Follow Microsoft's data protection guidelines and ensure compliance with local privacy laws (e.g., GDPR, CCPA).

By leveraging **Microsoft Copilot's API**, developers can create powerful, customized applications that harness the full potential of AI and automation within the **Microsoft 365** ecosystem. Whether you're enhancing productivity apps, developing AI-driven chatbots, or automating complex workflows, the possibilities with Copilot's API are vast and impactful for any developer.

CHAPTER SIX
SECURITY AND PRIVACY CONSIDERATIONS
Data Privacy Policies

When using **Microsoft Copilot** or integrating its AI capabilities into your applications, it's crucial to understand the **data privacy policies** to ensure compliance and protect users' data. Microsoft adheres to strict privacy standards, and its policies are designed to meet legal and regulatory requirements while offering transparency to users.

Below is an overview of the essential aspects of **data privacy** when working with Microsoft Copilot:

1. Microsoft's General Data Privacy Policy

Microsoft Copilot is governed by Microsoft's **Privacy Statement** and **Data Protection Terms**, which outline how data is collected, used, and protected. Microsoft is committed to transparency and protecting personal data while delivering AI-powered solutions.

- **Data Collection**: Microsoft collects data to power Copilot's functionality, but it takes steps to minimize unnecessary data collection.

- **Personal Data**: This includes personally identifiable information (PII), such as names, email addresses, and usage patterns, which may be collected when interacting with Microsoft 365 tools.

- **Data Usage**: Data collected through Copilot may be used to improve the AI's functionality, provide relevant suggestions, and personalize experiences for users. However, Microsoft offers customers control over how data is handled.

2. Data Processing and Compliance

Microsoft follows industry-standard data protection and privacy frameworks to ensure compliance with various regulations. These frameworks ensure that data is processed securely and that users' rights are respected.

- **General Data Protection Regulation (GDPR)**: Copilot follows the GDPR framework for users in the European Union (EU). This includes data subject rights, such as the right to access, correct, and delete personal data.

- **California Consumer Privacy Act (CCPA)**: For users in California, Microsoft ensures compliance with CCPA regulations, including providing transparency on how personal data is collected and giving users the right to opt-out of data sharing practices.

- **Other Regional Laws**: Microsoft Copilot also complies with other regional privacy laws, such as **Personal Data Protection Act (PDPA)** in Singapore, **Brazilian General Data Protection Law (LGPD)**, and **Australia's Privacy Act**.

3. Data Storage and Security

Microsoft uses its **Azure** infrastructure to store and secure data for Copilot, and robust security measures are in place to prevent unauthorized access or data breaches.

- **Encryption**: All data in transit and at rest is encrypted using industry-standard encryption protocols.

- **Data Anonymization**: In some cases, Copilot anonymizes or pseudonymizes data to prevent identifying individuals.

- **Access Control**: Access to user data is limited to authorized personnel and processes, ensuring that only those with legitimate business purposes can access sensitive information.

- **Multi-Factor Authentication (MFA)**: For added security, Microsoft recommends enabling MFA to secure your account, especially when accessing data through Microsoft 365 and Copilot.

4. Data Retention and Deletion

Microsoft offers flexible options for managing how long data is retained within Copilot and its associated Microsoft 365 services.

- **Retention Period**: The retention period varies depending on the type of data and the service. For example, **email data** in **Outlook** or **documents** in **Word** may be retained for different durations depending on user settings.

- **Deletion**: Users can delete documents, emails, and other data stored within Microsoft 365. In some cases, Microsoft allows users to delete data associated with Copilot's AI training or user interactions.

- **Right to Erasure**: Under GDPR and similar laws, users can request the deletion of their personal data stored by Microsoft, including data used by Copilot, which will be processed within the required time frame.

5. User Control and Transparency

Microsoft provides users with tools and settings to control what data is shared and how it is used by Copilot.

- **Privacy Settings**: Users can manage **privacy preferences** through Microsoft 365 settings, allowing them to opt-out of certain data-sharing practices or limit data collection.

- **Data Access and Correction**: Users can access their personal data collected through Copilot and other Microsoft services, and correct any inaccuracies via the privacy portal.

- **Data Sharing Preferences**: Users have the option to disable Copilot's AI features that require data sharing, ensuring that personal or sensitive information is not utilized by the system.

6. Third-Party Data Sharing and Integration

Microsoft's policy ensures that third-party applications and integrations with Copilot do not compromise user privacy.

- **API Data Handling**: When integrating third-party applications or APIs with Copilot, developers are responsible for ensuring that they comply with data privacy regulations and that they handle user data securely.

- **Third-Party Vendors**: Microsoft only shares data with third parties when necessary, such as through integrations with third-party services (e.g., Salesforce, Slack), and these third parties are bound by contractual agreements to safeguard user data.

7. AI Training and Model Updates

Copilot's AI models may be trained using anonymized and aggregated data to improve their performance. Microsoft takes care to ensure that individual user data is not misused during model updates.

- **Training Data**: Training data is typically anonymized to prevent the identification of individuals. Microsoft uses large, publicly available datasets and aggregated data from its services to train and fine-tune the models powering Copilot.

- **Model Updates**: Copilot's models are updated periodically to improve their performance and functionality. Users are notified about major updates through release notes, which include changes to data handling practices.

8. User Consent and Opt-Out

When using Microsoft Copilot, users may be required to give consent to the data collection and processing practices, particularly in cases where personal or sensitive data is involved.

- **Opt-Out Mechanisms**: Users can opt out of some features, like personalized suggestions or AI-driven document edits, if they do not wish to share their data with Copilot.

- **User Notifications**: Microsoft notifies users about any significant changes in its data privacy policies, providing clear instructions on how to manage consent.

9. Transparency and Audits

Microsoft encourages transparency in data practices and offers tools to help organizations track and manage their data use.

- **Audit Logs**: Microsoft offers audit logs for enterprise users to track data access and actions taken within Copilot and other Microsoft 365 services.

- **Transparency Reports**: Microsoft regularly publishes transparency reports that detail requests for data access from governments and third parties, ensuring accountability in data handling.

Microsoft Copilot adheres to stringent data privacy policies to protect user data, comply with global privacy laws, and give users control over their personal information.

By using Microsoft's comprehensive privacy settings and maintaining awareness of how their data is collected and used, users and developers can ensure that they are handling sensitive data responsibly while utilizing Copilot's AI features to enhance productivity and efficiency.

Security Measures and Compliance

When using Microsoft Copilot or integrating it into applications, security and compliance are critical aspects to ensure that your data is protected and that you're adhering to regulatory requirements. Microsoft implements a variety of security measures and compliance frameworks to safeguard data and ensure that Copilot meets the necessary standards for both enterprise and individual users.

1. Security Measures for Microsoft Copilot

Microsoft places a strong emphasis on securing user data and preventing unauthorized access, particularly in a cloud-based environment where sensitive information may be at risk. Below are the key security measures implemented by Microsoft for Copilot:

a. Data Encryption

- **Encryption at Rest**: All data stored within Microsoft 365 services, including data accessed or generated by Copilot, is encrypted using **AES-256** encryption. This ensures that even if the data is compromised, it remains unreadable without the encryption key.

- **Encryption in Transit**: Data transmitted between your device and Microsoft's servers is encrypted using **Transport Layer Security (TLS)**. This protects data from being intercepted during transmission.

b. Multi-Factor Authentication (MFA)

- Microsoft recommends enabling **MFA** to secure user accounts, especially for those accessing sensitive data or performing actions through Copilot. This adds an extra layer of security by requiring two or more verification methods (e.g., something you know, like a password, and something you have, like a mobile device).

- MFA is critical for preventing unauthorized access, particularly in high-risk environments.

c. Role-Based Access Control (RBAC)

- Microsoft uses **Role-Based Access Control** to manage permissions within Microsoft 365 services. This ensures that only authorized users or administrators can access or modify sensitive data.

- You can define and manage user roles and permissions within Microsoft Copilot to ensure that only specific team members or individuals have access to particular features or data.

d. Secure APIs

- Microsoft enforces security on all APIs interacting with Copilot, including the **Microsoft Graph API** and **Azure OpenAI Service API**. All API requests are subject to authorization and authentication to ensure that only authorized applications or users can interact with data.

- **OAuth 2.0** and **API keys** are used to control access to Copilot's API, ensuring secure data transactions.

e. Threat Detection and Monitoring

- Microsoft uses advanced **threat detection** tools, including machine learning models, to monitor for suspicious activities, breaches, and unauthorized access.

- **Microsoft Defender** and other security tools provide continuous monitoring of threats, ensuring any unusual activity is identified and acted upon swiftly.

f. Secure Cloud Infrastructure

- Copilot leverages Microsoft's **Azure Cloud** infrastructure, which is built with robust security protocols and features such as **firewalls**, **intrusion detection systems**, and **data loss**

prevention (DLP) tools. This infrastructure ensures that data is stored in secure, redundant data centers and protected from physical and cyber threats.

g. Secure Software Development Lifecycle (SDLC)

- Microsoft adheres to a **Secure Development Lifecycle (SDL)** when building Copilot. This involves incorporating security and privacy considerations throughout the development process, from design to deployment, and ensuring that vulnerabilities are identified and mitigated before release.

2. Compliance Frameworks for Microsoft Copilot

Microsoft is committed to ensuring that Copilot complies with a variety of **global data privacy and security regulations**. This compliance is essential for organizations that handle sensitive information, especially in highly regulated industries.

a. General Data Protection Regulation (GDPR)

- **GDPR** is a comprehensive data protection regulation that governs how businesses collect, store, and process personal data of EU citizens.

- Microsoft Copilot complies with GDPR by implementing strict data privacy and security protocols. This includes **data subject rights** such as the right to access, correct, delete, or port personal data.

- **Data Processing Agreement (DPA)**: For enterprise customers, Microsoft offers a DPA, which defines the terms under which personal data is processed, ensuring compliance with GDPR.

- **Cross-Border Data Transfers**: Microsoft ensures that data transfers across borders (such as from the EU to other regions) comply with GDPR's provisions on international data transfers.

b. California Consumer Privacy Act (CCPA)

- The **CCPA** provides privacy rights to California residents, including the right to know what personal data is being collected, the right to request deletion of data, and the right to opt-out of data selling.

- Microsoft Copilot offers features that allow users to manage their personal data preferences, including the ability to delete data or opt-out of data sharing.

- **Notice of Collection**: Users are notified when their data is collected, and Microsoft provides mechanisms to access or delete that data in compliance with the CCPA.

c. Health Insurance Portability and Accountability Act (HIPAA)

- **HIPAA** governs the use and disclosure of protected health information (PHI) in the U.S. If an organization uses Microsoft Copilot in a healthcare environment, Microsoft offers **HIPAA-compliant services**.

- Microsoft provides a **Business Associate Agreement (BAA)**, ensuring that PHI is processed securely, and the required privacy protections are in place for healthcare organizations.

d. Federal Risk and Authorization Management Program (FedRAMP)

- For U.S. federal agencies, **FedRAMP** compliance ensures that cloud services meet stringent security and privacy requirements.

- Microsoft has obtained **FedRAMP certifications** for many of its cloud services, including Microsoft 365, ensuring that Copilot is secure for use by federal agencies.

e. ISO/IEC 27001 Certification

- **ISO/IEC 27001** is an internationally recognized standard for information security management systems (ISMS).

- Microsoft's infrastructure, including services that support Copilot, is certified under this standard, demonstrating its commitment to securing sensitive data.

f. SOC 1, SOC 2, and SOC 3

- Microsoft provides **Service Organization Control (SOC)** reports, including **SOC 1**, **SOC 2**, and **SOC 3**, which are independent audits of its cloud services.

- These reports evaluate Microsoft's security, availability, confidentiality, processing integrity, and privacy practices, ensuring that Copilot meets high standards for handling sensitive data.

g. Data Localization Laws

- Microsoft Copilot complies with data localization laws, which require certain types of data to be stored in specific geographic regions. Microsoft's Azure data centers are distributed globally, allowing customers to choose the region where their data is stored and processed to meet local regulatory requirements.

3. User Responsibilities for Security and Compliance

While Microsoft provides strong security measures and ensures compliance with various regulations, users and organizations also have responsibilities to ensure the security and compliance of their data within Copilot:

a. Data Access and User Permissions

- Organizations should ensure that they configure user permissions and access controls correctly within Microsoft 365 to limit access to sensitive data.

- Implement **least privilege** access, where users only have the minimum permissions necessary to perform their tasks.

b. Regular Audits and Monitoring

- Organizations should regularly audit their use of Microsoft Copilot and associated services to ensure compliance with internal policies and external regulations.

- Microsoft provides **audit logs** and **security dashboards** to help administrators track activities within Copilot and other Microsoft 365 services.

c. Data Encryption and Backup

- While Microsoft handles encryption, organizations should also implement their own **encryption** for sensitive data before uploading it to Microsoft services.

- Regular **backups** should be performed to ensure data recovery in case of an incident.

d. Privacy and Data Retention Policies

- Organizations should establish and enforce clear **data retention policies** and ensure that data is not kept longer than necessary.

- Users should be given the option to **opt-out** of certain data collection practices or request data deletion, depending on the regulations in place.

Microsoft Copilot ensures that robust **security measures** and **compliance frameworks** are in place to protect user data and meet global privacy regulations. By leveraging encryption, authentication, and secure cloud infrastructure, Microsoft provides a secure platform for businesses and individuals to use AI-powered tools like Copilot.

At the same time, Microsoft's commitment to industry standards like GDPR, CCPA, and ISO certifications ensures that users' data remains secure and compliant with relevant laws and regulations. However, organizations and users must also take responsibility for their own data privacy and security configurations to ensure comprehensive protection.

Managing Permissions and Access

Effectively managing permissions and access to Microsoft Copilot and the associated Microsoft 365 tools is crucial to ensure that only authorized users can access sensitive data and perform specific tasks. Proper management helps protect organizational resources, maintain data privacy, and comply with relevant security regulations. Here's an overview of how to manage permissions and access in Microsoft Copilot:

1. Role-Based Access Control (RBAC)

Microsoft Copilot utilizes **Role-Based Access Control (RBAC)**, a framework that restricts system access to authorized users based on their role within an organization. By using RBAC, administrators can control which users can perform certain actions within Microsoft 365 and Copilot.

How RBAC Works:

- **Roles** are assigned to users, each with specific permissions.

- Permissions determine which actions a user can perform, such as accessing data, editing documents, or managing Copilot settings.

- **Admin roles** are typically assigned to IT professionals or team leaders, while **user roles** may have more limited access depending on their job responsibilities.

Common RBAC Roles in Microsoft 365 and Copilot:

- **Global Administrator**: Has full access to all settings, including user management, security settings, and Copilot configurations.

- **User Administrator**: Can manage users and their permissions but has limited access to Copilot-specific settings.

- **Compliance Administrator**: Manages compliance features and data retention settings.

- **Helpdesk Administrator**: Limited to user support functions but cannot alter Copilot configurations or access sensitive data.

- **Standard User**: Has access to Copilot features for day-to-day tasks, like document creation or email management, based on permissions granted.

2. Managing Permissions via Microsoft 365 Admin Center

Microsoft provides the **Microsoft 365 Admin Center** as the central hub for managing permissions and access across its suite of services, including Copilot.

Steps to Manage Permissions:

1. **Log into the Admin Center**: Visit the Microsoft 365 Admin Center at admin.microsoft.com and sign in with your administrator credentials.

2. **Navigate to Roles**: Under the **Admin Centers** section, go to **Roles** to view and manage the roles assigned to users.

3. **Assign Roles**: Choose a role from the list and assign it to a user or group, depending on their function within your organization.

4. **Customize Permissions**: For more granular control, you can adjust permissions related to specific services like **Outlook**, **OneDrive**, or **SharePoint** that integrate with Copilot.

5. **Manage Access to Copilot**: In the case of Copilot-specific settings, permissions can be set via the **Copilot settings** within the Admin Center, which allows administrators to grant or restrict access to Copilot's AI-powered features, such as content suggestions, document editing, and data analysis.

Key Actions in the Admin Center:

- **Assign Users to Groups**: Grouping users by department or function helps streamline permission management. For example, a group of content creators can be granted specific permissions related to editing and suggesting content, while a group of administrators has broader access.

- **Set Up Security Groups**: Microsoft allows you to set up **security groups** for different purposes. For instance, you might have a security group that can access sensitive documents processed by Copilot, while others have more limited access.

- **Monitor User Activity**: Administrators can monitor which users are using Copilot features and track their access levels, ensuring compliance with internal security policies.

3. Access Permissions for Copilot Features

Access to Microsoft Copilot's capabilities can be managed and restricted based on specific features or tools within the Microsoft 365 suite, such as Word, Excel, and Outlook.

Key Permissions for Copilot Features:

- **Content Creation and Editing**: Users can be given access to Copilot's ability to generate content (e.g., drafting text in Word or creating presentations in PowerPoint). This can be restricted based on roles.

- **AI Suggestions**: Permissions can be granted for users to receive AI-based suggestions, including grammar corrections, style improvements, and other content enhancements.

- **Analytics and Insights**: Administrators may choose to grant or restrict access to Copilot's data insights and analytics features. These capabilities may require higher-level permissions for security or regulatory reasons.

- **Automation of Tasks**: Copilot's ability to automate repetitive tasks (e.g., generating reports, sending emails, etc.) can be configured based on user roles. For example, only specific users might have the ability to create and deploy automation workflows.

4. Managing Permissions for Data Sharing and Collaboration

Microsoft Copilot enables collaboration and sharing within documents and teams. Properly managing permissions in these areas is essential for maintaining control over sensitive information.

Managing Sharing Permissions in Microsoft 365:

- **SharePoint and OneDrive**: When using Copilot within SharePoint or OneDrive, administrators can control who has access to shared documents, folders, and teams. Share permissions can be granted at the document level or for entire folders.

- **Teams**: For Copilot-powered features in Microsoft Teams, permissions for sharing files, collaborating on content, and using Copilot's AI-based tools can be controlled. Administrators can manage who can use Copilot's chat and collaboration features within Teams channels.

- **External Sharing**: Control the ability to share documents or data with external users (e.g., clients or partners). This is typically disabled or restricted by default to ensure data security.

5. Using Microsoft Compliance Center to Manage Data Access

For organizations with more advanced compliance needs, Microsoft offers the **Microsoft Compliance Center**. This tool allows for fine-grained control over how data is managed, tracked, and accessed, which can directly affect Copilot's usage.

Features for Managing Data Access:

- **Information Governance**: Set policies for data retention, ensuring that sensitive data is deleted after a certain period.

- **Data Loss Prevention (DLP)**: Create DLP policies to prevent sensitive information from being shared or accessed inappropriately. This is especially useful for sensitive documents or communications generated using Copilot.

- **eDiscovery and Auditing**: Use eDiscovery tools to search through data and track access events, ensuring compliance with legal and regulatory requirements.

6. Conditional Access Policies

Microsoft provides **Conditional Access** policies to ensure that users can only access Copilot and other Microsoft 365 services under specific conditions. This helps protect data and systems from unauthorized access, especially when users are working remotely or accessing from less secure devices.

Examples of Conditional Access:

- **Location-Based Access**: Grant or block access to Copilot based on the user's geographic location.

- **Device Compliance**: Ensure that users accessing Copilot are using compliant devices (e.g., devices with up-to-date security patches).

- **Risk-Based Access**: If a user's sign-in activity appears risky (e.g., multiple failed login attempts), access to Copilot can be temporarily blocked or require additional authentication.

7. Auditing and Monitoring Access to Copilot

Administrators can monitor and audit who is accessing Microsoft Copilot and what actions they are performing. This includes tracking **user logins**, **document edits**, and **AI suggestions** provided by Copilot.

Audit Logs:

- Administrators can access audit logs to track Copilot-related activities. This includes which users requested AI suggestions, which documents were modified, and any other Copilot actions that might require oversight.

- Audit logs are essential for compliance reporting and detecting any unauthorized or unusual activity.

Managing permissions and access to Microsoft Copilot is vital for ensuring security, data privacy, and compliance within your organization. By utilizing **Role-Based Access Control (RBAC)**, **Microsoft 365 Admin Center**, and **Compliance Center** tools, administrators can control access to Copilot's AI-powered features and data.

Setting up proper **sharing permissions**, **conditional access policies**, and regular **audits** ensures that sensitive data is protected while maximizing the benefits of Copilot. By doing so, organizations can effectively maintain security and compliance while enhancing productivity and collaboration with Microsoft Copilot.

CHAPTER SEVEN
TROUBLESHOOTING AND SUPPORT

Common Issues and Solutions

Microsoft Copilot, while powerful and intuitive, may present occasional challenges for users. Here are some of the most common issues that users may encounter, along with practical solutions to resolve them:

1. Copilot Not Responding or Loading

Issue:

Copilot may fail to load or respond when you try to use it, leaving users unable to access its features in Microsoft applications.

Possible Causes:

- **Network connectivity issues**: Slow or unstable internet connections can hinder Copilot's performance.

- **Service outages**: Copilot may be down due to service maintenance or unexpected outages.

- **Browser or software issues**: Copilot may not function properly if the browser or software is outdated.

Solution:

- **Check Internet Connection**: Ensure your internet connection is stable and fast enough to support cloud-based services.

- **Visit Microsoft's Service Health Page**: Check the Microsoft 365 Service Health Dashboard to see if there are any ongoing outages or issues with Copilot or other services.

- **Clear Cache and Cookies**: Clear the cache and cookies from your browser if using web-based apps like Word or Excel. This can often resolve loading issues.

- **Update Software**: Ensure that the applications you're using are up to date (Microsoft Word, Excel, PowerPoint, etc.).

- **Restart the Application**: Try restarting the application (e.g., Microsoft Word, Excel) or the entire computer to resolve temporary glitches.

2. Inaccurate or Unhelpful Suggestions

Issue:

Copilot may provide suggestions that are irrelevant or do not align with your expectations, leading to poor user experience.

Possible Causes:

- **Lack of data context**: Copilot may not have enough context to provide relevant suggestions, especially if the document or data is incomplete.

- **Misconfigured preferences**: Personalized settings and preferences may not be set correctly, resulting in suggestions that don't match your needs.

Solution:

- **Provide More Context**: Ensure that you are providing Copilot with enough context in the document or query. For example, if working on a report, provide background information or details about the desired outcome.

- **Refine Prompts**: When interacting with Copilot (especially in Word or Excel), be more specific in your instructions or queries. Copilot responds better to detailed commands.

- **Adjust Settings and Preferences**: Go to **Copilot settings** and customize its behavior. Make sure the AI has access to relevant data and adjust your personal preferences for suggestions.

- **Give Feedback**: Copilot may improve over time with user feedback. If suggestions are consistently unhelpful, you can provide feedback to help Microsoft refine the AI's capabilities.

3. Copilot Not Accessing or Editing Documents Correctly

Issue:

Copilot might struggle to access or edit certain documents, especially in collaborative environments or with files stored in cloud services.

Possible Causes:

- **File Permissions**: Copilot may not have the necessary permissions to access or edit documents, especially in shared environments.

- **Cloud Syncing Issues**: Documents stored in cloud services like OneDrive or SharePoint may not sync correctly, preventing Copilot from accessing the latest version of the document.

- **Outdated Versions**: Copilot might be interacting with an outdated version of a document, which may cause issues with editing or suggesting improvements.

Solution:

- **Check Document Permissions**: Ensure that the document is shared with the correct users and that Copilot has permission to access and edit the file.

- **Verify Cloud Syncing**: Make sure the document is correctly synced with cloud storage (OneDrive or SharePoint). If necessary, force a sync to update the file.

- **Open the Latest Version**: Double-check that you are working with the latest version of the document and that all changes are reflected in the cloud-based version.

4. Issues with Copilot Integration with Other Microsoft 365 Apps

Issue:

Copilot may not integrate seamlessly with other Microsoft 365 apps, such as Teams, SharePoint, or OneDrive, leading to functionality issues.

Possible Causes:

- **App Version Mismatch**: If some Microsoft apps are not updated to the latest version, integration with Copilot may fail or be limited.

- **API or Service Interruptions**: If an API or service interruption occurs, Copilot might not be able to interact with other Microsoft 365 apps.

Solution:

- **Update All Microsoft 365 Apps**: Ensure all Microsoft 365 apps (Word, Excel, PowerPoint, Teams, etc.) are updated to the latest versions.

- **Check Permissions and Access**: Verify that Copilot has the necessary permissions to interact with other Microsoft services, such as Teams or SharePoint. This may involve adjusting settings within the Microsoft 365 Admin Center.

- **Test Integration with Other Tools**: If integration with a third-party app is causing issues, review the integration settings, and ensure that the tools and APIs are functioning correctly.

5. Copilot Not Offering Relevant Data Insights or Analytics

Issue:

Users may experience problems when trying to get data insights or analytics from Copilot, especially in applications like Excel or Power BI.

Possible Causes:

- **Data Quality**: Copilot needs structured, clean, and organized data to provide accurate insights. Unorganized or incomplete data can lead to poor results.

- **Permissions Issues**: Copilot may not have the necessary permissions to access certain data sources or may be limited by access control policies.

Solution:

- **Ensure Data is Well-Structured**: For Copilot to provide accurate insights, make sure the data in Excel, Power BI, or other apps is well-organized. Clean up any errors, missing values, or inconsistencies.

- **Check Permissions**: Ensure that Copilot has access to the data it needs. This might involve adjusting settings in Power BI, Excel, or SharePoint to allow Copilot to interact with specific data sources.

- **Use Guided Suggestions**: If insights are not appearing as expected, try using more specific queries or prompts, asking Copilot for insights on particular trends or analysis areas.

6. Copilot AI Suggestion Delays

Issue:

Copilot may take a long time to process or provide suggestions, especially in larger documents or datasets.

Possible Causes:

- **Large Files**: Copilot may experience delays when working with very large files or datasets.

- **Server Load**: High traffic or server load from other users may cause delays in Copilot's response times.

Solution:

- **Optimize Document Size**: If possible, break large documents into smaller files or reduce the complexity of data in Excel. This can help Copilot process requests more efficiently.

- **Wait for Server Load to Decrease**: If Copilot is slow due to server load, the best solution is often to wait for some time or try again later.

- **Use Offline Features**: For basic tasks that don't require Copilot, try completing the task without relying on its AI features to avoid delays.

7. Copilot Misunderstanding Commands or Requests

Issue:

Copilot may not understand complex commands or misinterpret user instructions, leading to inaccurate results.

Possible Causes:

- **Vague or Ambiguous Commands**: Copilot's natural language processing capabilities rely on clear, precise inputs. Ambiguous or overly complex instructions can confuse the AI.

- **Limited Training Data**: If Copilot hasn't been trained on specific types of tasks or content, it may not provide the expected results.

Solution:

- **Be Specific**: When issuing commands, be as specific as possible. For example, instead of asking Copilot to "analyze the data," specify what type of analysis you want, such as "identify trends in sales data over the past six months."

- **Refine Instructions**: If Copilot doesn't understand your request, try breaking it down into smaller, more manageable tasks or restate your request in simpler terms.

Microsoft Copilot is a sophisticated tool that enhances productivity through AI-powered features, but like any advanced technology, users may encounter common issues. These problems can often be resolved by addressing issues such as connectivity, permissions, and data quality. By following the solutions outlined above, users can minimize disruptions and fully leverage Copilot's capabilities.

Accessing Support Resources

If you encounter issues or need help while using Microsoft Copilot, there are several support resources available to ensure a smooth experience. Here's how to access support:

1. Microsoft Support Website

- **Website**: Visit the official Microsoft Support website for comprehensive help and troubleshooting guides.

- **How to Use**: You can search for specific issues, such as "Copilot not responding" or "AI suggestions in Word not working," and find relevant articles, troubleshooting steps, and solutions.

2. In-App Support

- **How to Access**:

    o Open the **Help** menu in Microsoft applications (e.g., Word, Excel, PowerPoint).

    o Select **Get Help** or **Contact Support** from the options.

    o You can also use the **?" icon in the upper-right corner of the app to search for assistance.

- **Features**:

    o **Chatbot Assistance**: The support system includes a chatbot for answering basic questions or providing initial troubleshooting tips.

    o **Live Support**: You can also schedule a live chat or phone call with a support agent if the chatbot cannot resolve the issue.

3. Microsoft 365 Admin Center (for Admins)

- **How to Access**:

    o Admins can log in to the Microsoft 365 Admin Center.

    o Navigate to the **Support** section, where you can get access to resources like service health, troubleshooting guides, and support ticket management.

- **Features**:

    o **Service Health**: Check for any ongoing issues or outages related to Microsoft Copilot or other services.

    o **Submit a Support Ticket**: If your issue is unresolved, admins can submit a support ticket and track its progress.

4. Microsoft Community Forums

- **Website**: Microsoft Community

- **How to Use**: Search for topics related to Copilot or post questions about issues you're experiencing.

- **Features**:
    - **Community Answers**: Other users may have had similar issues and can offer solutions.
    - **Official Microsoft Moderators**: Occasionally, Microsoft experts participate in discussions, providing guidance and help.

5. Help and Training Videos

- **How to Access**: On the Microsoft Support site or directly in the app, you can access tutorials and training videos that walk you through specific features and troubleshooting steps.

- **Features**:
    - **Step-by-Step Guides**: Detailed guides and videos for common Copilot tasks.
    - **Interactive Tutorials**: Some features include interactive tutorials that allow you to practice using Copilot in real-time.

6. Copilot Help Menu (Inside the App)

- **How to Access**:
    - Inside any Microsoft 365 app (e.g., Word, Excel, PowerPoint), you can access Copilot-specific help by clicking on the **Copilot icon** or navigating to **Help** > **Copilot Help**.
    - This will provide tips, use case examples, and direct links to Microsoft resources or FAQs related to Copilot.

7. Copilot Updates and Documentation

- **Website**: Visit Microsoft's Copilot Documentation page for official release notes, technical guides, and in-depth documentation.

- **Features**:
    - **Release Notes**: Keep up with new features, bug fixes, and updates to Copilot.
    - **Developer Resources**: For those using Copilot in conjunction with custom APIs or third-party applications, Microsoft provides developer-specific documentation.

8. Contacting Microsoft Support Directly

- **Phone or Chat Support**: If you cannot resolve your issue with self-help resources, Microsoft offers direct customer support via phone or chat.

- **How to Access**: You can initiate this by visiting the Microsoft Support website and navigating to the **Contact Support** section.

9. Troubleshooting Tools

- **Microsoft Support and Recovery Assistant**: This tool can help diagnose and fix issues with Microsoft 365 apps, including Copilot, by automatically detecting and resolving common problems.

- **How to Use**: Download the tool from the Microsoft Support and Recovery Assistant page, and follow the prompts to run a diagnostic check.

10. Social Media Channels

- **Microsoft Twitter**: Follow <u>Microsoft Support on Twitter</u> for the latest updates and troubleshooting tips.

- **Microsoft Community on Reddit**: The <u>Microsoft subreddit</u> is also a useful resource for discussions, tips, and common problems shared by users.

To resolve issues quickly and get the most out of Microsoft Copilot, you can rely on a combination of official support resources, community forums, and in-app help. If necessary, you can also contact Microsoft's dedicated customer service team for more personalized assistance.

Community and Forums

Engaging with community platforms and forums can be a great way to resolve issues, share experiences, and learn new tips for using Microsoft Copilot. Here's an overview of where you can find community-driven support and discussions about Copilot:

1. Microsoft Community

- **Website**: <u>Microsoft Community</u>
- **How to Use**:
  - Search for topics related to Microsoft Copilot or post questions if you're experiencing issues or have suggestions.
  - Browse the **Copilot** or **Microsoft 365** categories to find answers or start new discussions.
- **Features**:
  - **Community Answers**: Many users share their solutions to common problems, which can help you troubleshoot.
  - **Official Microsoft Moderators**: Microsoft employees occasionally participate in discussions, providing authoritative solutions or clarifications.
  - **Helpful Tags**: Tag your posts with relevant keywords (like "Copilot" or "AI Suggestions") to make them easier for others to find.

2. Microsoft Tech Community

- **Website**: <u>Microsoft Tech Community</u>
- **How to Use**:
  - Join the **Microsoft Copilot** or **Microsoft 365** groups within the Tech Community to discuss Copilot's features, share feedback, and explore technical insights.
  - Participate in **Q&A discussions**, post your questions, or share solutions to challenges.

- **Features**:
    - o **Product and Feature Discussions**: These communities allow you to dive deeper into specific features of Microsoft products, including Copilot, and discuss its functionality.
    - o **Tech Experts**: Engage with Microsoft engineers, MVPs (Most Valuable Professionals), and experienced users for more advanced insights.
    - o **Live Events and Webinars**: Attend webinars and live events to learn about new features, best practices, and Copilot updates.

3. Reddit - Microsoft Subreddits

- **Subreddits**:
    - o r/Microsoft
    - o r/Microsoft365
    - o r/Office365

- **How to Use**:
    - o These subreddits are filled with discussions related to Microsoft products, including Copilot. You can search for threads on Copilot or post your own question.
    - o Share experiences, learn from other users, and discuss new features or bugs.

- **Features**:
    - o **User-Led Discussions**: Join conversations with fellow users about Copilot, share tips, or seek advice.
    - o **Frequent Updates**: These subreddits often feature discussions about the latest Copilot features and updates.
    - o **Helpful Feedback**: Users often share workarounds, tips, and hacks for maximizing Copilot's potential.

4. Stack Overflow

- **Website**: Stack Overflow
- **How to Use**:
    - o If you're a developer integrating Copilot with third-party applications or using its API, Stack Overflow is a valuable resource for technical support.
    - o Search for questions related to Copilot or post your own development-related query.
- **Features**:
    - o **Developer-Centric**: Focuses on coding, integration, and technical aspects of Copilot.
    - o **Expert Advice**: Get help from experienced developers and Copilot experts.
    - o **Code Examples and Best Practices**: Find examples and learn best practices for using Copilot's API.

5. Microsoft Feedback Hub

- **Website**: Microsoft Feedback Hub

- **How to Use**:

  - For Windows users, the **Feedback Hub** is a great place to report bugs, share your experiences, or suggest improvements related to Copilot.

  - You can post feedback or upvote suggestions from other users that are relevant to Copilot.

- **Features**:

  - **Direct Feedback**: Provide feedback directly to Microsoft about Copilot and other Microsoft 365 features.

  - **Track Feature Requests**: See if others have requested the same feature or issue, and track updates from Microsoft.

  - **Vote on Ideas**: Vote for ideas or solutions you believe should be prioritized by the development team.

6. Microsoft UserVoice (Legacy)

- **Website**: UserVoice for Microsoft

- **How to Use**:

  - Although Microsoft has been transitioning away from UserVoice, some legacy forums and product-specific feedback channels still exist where you can voice your opinions and ideas on Copilot.

  - Check for ongoing feedback forums related to Microsoft products, including Copilot.

- **Features**:

  - **Submit Feature Requests**: Suggest new features or improvements for Copilot.

  - **Upvote Ideas**: Vote for ideas and suggestions submitted by other users.

7. Copilot-Specific Forums (Upcoming)

- **How to Use**:

  - As Copilot becomes more integrated into Microsoft 365, Microsoft may establish new dedicated Copilot forums and support communities.

  - Keep an eye on official announcements and updates for new spaces for discussions specifically focused on Copilot.

- **Features**:

  - **Focused Copilot Discussions**: These forums would likely allow you to find specific topics related to Copilot's features, troubleshooting, or feedback.

8. Microsoft Developer Network (MSDN) Forums

- **Website**: MSDN Forums

- **How to Use**:

  - Developers integrating Copilot into custom applications or exploring its API can ask technical questions here.

  - Search for topics related to Copilot's API or integration with other services.

- **Features**:

  - **Technical Community**: Get help from developers, including answers to Copilot API-related queries.

  - **In-Depth Discussions**: Participate in detailed discussions around development and troubleshooting for Copilot integrations.

9. Discord Communities

- **How to Use**:

  - Look for unofficial Discord servers or community spaces where Microsoft users gather to discuss Copilot and other Microsoft tools.

- **Features**:

  - **Real-Time Chat**: Participate in fast-paced, real-time conversations about Copilot.

  - **Collaborative Support**: Get instant support from fellow users, share ideas, or help others.

Benefits of Community and Forums:

- **Peer Support**: Many common issues with Copilot are resolved by the community, which can often offer quick, practical solutions.

- **Feature Exploration**: Communities are great places to discuss new features, beta updates, and best practices.

- **Learning**: Interacting with other users or developers can help you learn creative ways to use Copilot in your workflow.

- **Feedback and Suggestions**: Engage with other users and provide feedback to Microsoft, helping to shape future updates to Copilot.

By tapping into these community resources, you can enhance your Microsoft Copilot experience, troubleshoot common issues, and stay up to date with new features and best practices.

CHAPTER EIGHT
BEST PRACTICES FOR MAXIMIZING PRODUCTIVITY

Tips and Tricks

Here are some valuable tips and tricks to help you maximize your use of Microsoft Copilot in 2025, whether you're using it for work, productivity, or content creation:

1. Leverage Copilot for Document Drafting

- **Tip**: Use Copilot to help you create drafts for reports, emails, or presentations. Simply provide a brief description of what you want, and Copilot can generate text based on your instructions.

- **Trick**: If you want to adjust the tone (e.g., more formal or casual), specify it in your prompt. Copilot will tailor the language accordingly.

2. Create Custom Templates

- **Tip**: In Microsoft Word and PowerPoint, use Copilot to create custom document and slide templates. You can specify your design preferences (e.g., color schemes, layout, and structure) and Copilot will generate a personalized template.

- **Trick**: After generating a template, save it in your templates library for future use.

3. Use Copilot for Data Analysis in Excel

- **Tip**: Copilot can help you analyze data by suggesting formulas, visualizations (like charts), and even summarizing large datasets.

- **Trick**: If you're working with a large dataset, ask Copilot to identify trends, correlations, or outliers. This can save you hours of analysis time.

- **Advanced Trick**: Use Copilot to generate PivotTables and advanced formulas by simply asking, e.g., "Can you create a PivotTable for this dataset that shows sales by region?"

4. Quickly Summarize Long Documents

- **Tip**: Copilot can summarize long Word documents, emails, or even web pages. Just ask, "Can you summarize this document?" to get a concise overview.

- **Trick**: Specify key points you want the summary to focus on, such as dates, people, or specific topics, for more targeted results.

5. Automate Routine Email Responses

- **Tip**: If you receive frequent emails with similar requests, you can set up templates or ask Copilot to generate email responses.

- **Trick**: Use Copilot's AI-powered suggestions to craft personalized replies quickly, and add your touch by reviewing and editing the content before sending.

6. Integrate Copilot with Microsoft Teams

- **Tip**: Use Copilot in Microsoft Teams to help with meeting notes, action item tracking, or brainstorming sessions. You can ask Copilot to generate summaries of discussions or suggest action points after a meeting.

- **Trick**: Copilot can also help with content creation for Teams chats, such as drafting messages or responses based on the conversation's context.

7. Translate Text with Copilot

- **Tip**: Copilot can help translate text in Word, Excel, and PowerPoint across various languages. Simply highlight the text you want to translate and ask Copilot to do it for you.

- **Trick**: Specify the tone or formality level for the translation, especially in business contexts.

8. Personalize Copilot's Suggestions

- **Tip**: Copilot offers suggestions based on your work patterns. Use this feature to customize its suggestions by providing feedback when it offers a suggestion you like or don't like.

- **Trick**: Train Copilot by continuing to use it in specific ways so it learns your preferences and can make better suggestions over time. The more you interact with Copilot, the better it becomes at predicting what you need.

9. Utilize Copilot for Meeting Scheduling in Outlook

- **Tip**: Use Copilot to help schedule meetings directly from your email or calendar. Just ask Copilot to find available time slots based on your calendar and preferences.

- **Trick**: Ask Copilot to send out meeting invites and even draft an agenda based on the discussion or topics you mention in the email.

10. Access Data-Driven Insights in Excel

- **Tip**: When working with financial or sales data in Excel, Copilot can help you gain insights by suggesting key performance indicators (KPIs) or analyzing trends.

- **Trick**: Ask Copilot to automatically generate forecasts or trendlines using your historical data. This can be a quick way to visualize future trends.

11. Write Creative Content with Copilot in PowerPoint

- **Tip**: Use Copilot to draft slide content for your presentations. You can give it bullet points or a general idea, and Copilot will turn them into polished slides.

- **Trick**: Ask Copilot for suggestions on the visual design of your slides (e.g., color schemes, font styles) to ensure your presentation is both informative and visually appealing.

12. Simplify Complex Ideas with Copilot

- **Tip**: If you're working with a complex idea or subject matter, ask Copilot to simplify it for easier understanding. Copilot can help you create definitions or break down complicated concepts into simpler language.

- **Trick**: Copilot can help rephrase content to match the knowledge level of your audience, whether it's for beginners or experts.

13. Real-Time Collaboration with Copilot

- **Tip**: In collaborative environments, Copilot can assist multiple users working on the same document by suggesting edits, clarifications, or grammar improvements.

- **Trick**: Use Copilot to coordinate inputs in real-time during a team brainstorming session, helping everyone stay aligned and efficient.

14. Use Voice Commands for Hands-Free Work

- **Tip**: In apps that support it, like Microsoft Word or PowerPoint, use voice commands to interact with Copilot, such as dictating content or issuing commands for formatting.

- **Trick**: Enable the "Dictate" feature in Microsoft 365 apps to let Copilot transcribe your voice into text and follow up with editing commands.

15. Monitor Progress with Copilot

- **Tip**: Use Copilot to track the progress of projects, tasks, or goals in apps like Excel or Microsoft Planner. You can ask it to generate reports, track deadlines, and monitor progress.

- **Trick**: Ask Copilot to generate visual progress reports, such as Gantt charts or completion percentages, to help you keep projects on track.

16. Stay Organized with Copilot's Task Management

- **Tip**: Use Copilot to manage your to-do lists in Outlook or Microsoft Planner. You can ask it to create tasks, set reminders, or categorize them based on priority.

- **Trick**: Let Copilot automatically suggest tasks based on emails or meetings that you have in your calendar.

17. Enhance Learning and Knowledge Acquisition

- **Tip**: Use Copilot to help with research. For example, it can gather information on specific topics, summarize articles, or create outlines for reports.

- **Trick**: Ask Copilot to curate relevant resources or provide citations if you're writing research papers or reports.

18. Minimize Errors with Copilot's Proofreading Capabilities

- **Tip**: Use Copilot to proofread your documents for spelling, grammar, and style errors. It can even provide suggestions for improving clarity and readability.

- **Trick**: Set the writing style (e.g., academic, business, casual) so that Copilot provides suggestions in the tone appropriate for your audience.

By using these tips and tricks, you can unlock the full potential of Microsoft Copilot, making your work more efficient, creative, and productive.

Case Studies and Success Stories

As Microsoft Copilot continues to revolutionize how users interact with Microsoft 365, there are numerous success stories across different industries that showcase the benefits of using AI-powered assistance for productivity, efficiency, and innovation. Below are a few case studies from various sectors:

Case Study: Enhancing Productivity in a Global Marketing Agency

Company: Global Marketing Agency (GMA)
Industry: Marketing and Advertising
Challenge: GMA faced challenges in managing large volumes of client content, campaign reporting, and creative collaboration across multiple teams. The agency needed a way to streamline its workflow, particularly in drafting client reports, presentations, and coordinating between departments.

Solution:

GMA integrated Microsoft Copilot with Microsoft Word, PowerPoint, and Excel to automate repetitive tasks like content drafting, report generation, and analysis. Copilot helped generate initial drafts for proposals and presentations based on the input data, saving the team significant time in content creation.

Results:

- **Time Savings**: Team members saved an average of 3-4 hours per week, as Copilot helped in drafting content and generating reports.

- **Increased Client Satisfaction**: With Copilot generating more polished drafts and reports, the agency delivered higher-quality work to clients in less time.

- **Streamlined Collaboration**: Teams were able to use Copilot's collaborative features in Microsoft Teams to create and share presentations, proposals, and reports in real-time, improving team cohesion and client-facing output.

Case Study: Optimizing Financial Analysis in a Financial Services Firm

Company: Financial Services Firm (FSF)
Industry: Financial Services
Challenge: The firm was managing vast amounts of financial data daily. Analysts needed to generate insights quickly from complex datasets, but manual processes were taking too long, leading to slower decision-making and missed opportunities for clients.

Solution:

FSF integrated Microsoft Copilot with Excel to automate financial modeling, data analysis, and reporting. Copilot suggested trends, correlations, and anomalies within data sets and even created data visualizations, like graphs and charts, based on the firm's financial data.

Results:

- **Faster Data Insights**: Analysts were able to generate reports 50% faster with Copilot's help, allowing them to focus more on strategic decision-making.

- **Improved Accuracy**: Copilot's AI suggestions helped eliminate errors in complex formulas and financial models, leading to more accurate financial reports.

- **Increased Productivity**: Analysts could handle more client requests and provide quicker turnaround times for financial assessments.

Case Study: Streamlining Operations in a Healthcare Organization

Company: Leading Healthcare Provider (LHP)
Industry: Healthcare

Challenge: The organization faced challenges in managing patient information, communications between staff, and scheduling. The manual input of patient data, appointment scheduling, and medical report generation were time-consuming, leading to delays in patient care and lower staff productivity.

Solution:
LHP deployed Microsoft Copilot in Microsoft Outlook and Word to automate appointment scheduling, create patient reports, and assist in communication between medical staff. Copilot helped streamline the process by suggesting appointment slots based on physicians' availability and assisting with the drafting of medical reports.

Results:

- **Reduced Administrative Work**: The staff saved up to 5 hours per week on administrative tasks, allowing more focus on patient care.

- **Improved Patient Experience**: With quicker scheduling and automated reminders, patients experienced fewer delays and more seamless communication with healthcare providers.

- **Increased Staff Efficiency**: The integration of Copilot's capabilities into Outlook and Word improved operational workflows and reduced workload burdens on staff, leading to greater overall productivity.

Case Study: Revolutionizing Product Development in a Tech Startup

Company: InnovTech Solutions (Tech Startup)
Industry: Technology and Software Development

Challenge: InnovTech's product development team struggled with time-consuming documentation tasks, code review processes, and project management. The team needed a solution to increase speed without sacrificing quality or accuracy in the development process.

Solution:
InnovTech utilized Microsoft Copilot in Visual Studio Code (VS Code) to assist with code review, documentation, and task management in Microsoft Teams. Copilot helped the team by reviewing code for potential bugs, suggesting improvements, and assisting in generating technical documentation for their software products.

Results:

- **Faster Development Cycles**: By reducing the time spent on documentation and bug detection, the development team could deploy new features 40% faster.

- **Improved Code Quality**: Copilot's real-time code suggestions and error detection helped catch potential issues early in the development process, improving the overall quality of the code.

- **Enhanced Collaboration**: Copilot facilitated smoother communication between development and product teams through automatic updates and collaborative features in Microsoft Teams.

Case Study: Revolutionizing Educational Content Creation in a University

Institution: National University (NU)

Industry: Higher Education

Challenge: Faculty at NU faced challenges in creating engaging course content, grading assignments, and offering timely feedback. The process was time-consuming and often led to delays in course updates and student assessments.

Solution:

The university implemented Microsoft Copilot in Word and Excel to streamline course material creation and automate grading processes. Copilot assisted in creating course syllabi, assignments, and quizzes, and also provided recommendations for student feedback based on grading patterns.

Results:

- **Increased Instructor Productivity**: Faculty members saved an average of 6 hours per week by automating repetitive tasks like creating quizzes and grading assignments.

- **Improved Student Feedback**: Students received more timely feedback, which led to an increase in student satisfaction and engagement.

- **Enhanced Course Design**: Copilot provided insights into how to improve course content by suggesting enhancements and offering real-time student performance analytics.

Microsoft Copilot is transforming industries by automating time-consuming tasks, improving productivity, and enhancing collaboration across departments. These case studies showcase how businesses, educational institutions, healthcare providers, and tech startups are leveraging AI-powered tools to achieve faster results, improved accuracy, and better decision-making.

Whether it's streamlining administrative tasks, enhancing content creation, or optimizing complex analyses, Microsoft Copilot is proving to be an invaluable asset in the modern workplace.

Continuous Learning and Updates

Microsoft Copilot is designed to evolve constantly, ensuring that users benefit from the latest advancements in AI, productivity tools, and Microsoft 365 apps. To maximize the effectiveness of Copilot and stay ahead of new features, it's crucial to engage in continuous learning and take advantage of regular updates. Below are some essential strategies and practices for staying current with Microsoft Copilot's capabilities:

1. Regularly Review New Features and Updates

- **Why**: Microsoft continuously enhances Copilot's features to improve its functionality and user experience. New tools, integrations, or capabilities are introduced frequently.

- **How**:

    - Monitor the official Microsoft 365 update page, where Microsoft announces new features, improvements, and changes.

- Enable automatic updates for Microsoft 365 apps to ensure you're always on the latest version with the most up-to-date Copilot features.

- **Tip**: Subscribe to Microsoft's newsletters or follow their official social media channels to stay informed about the latest product updates.

2. Participate in Training and Webinars

- **Why**: Microsoft frequently offers online training, webinars, and courses to help users understand and leverage new features within Copilot and Microsoft 365 apps.

- **How**:

  - Check the Microsoft Learn platform for free courses tailored to Copilot's functionality.

  - Attend webinars hosted by Microsoft or certified training partners to dive deeper into new features and best practices.

- **Tip**: After attending a training session, experiment with new features and tools to practice using them and incorporate them into your workflows.

3. Access Copilot's Built-in Learning Tools

- **Why**: Copilot itself is a learning tool. It provides suggestions and insights tailored to your specific work habits, and it can be a valuable resource for learning on the fly.

- **How**:

  - Engage with Copilot's suggestions in real-time as you work. When Copilot suggests features or automations, take a moment to understand how they function.

  - Use the "Learn More" or "Help" options within Copilot to get detailed explanations about new functionalities.

- **Tip**: Ask Copilot specific questions to understand its capabilities more thoroughly. For instance, you can say, "What new features are available for automation in Excel?" to receive information about recent updates.

4. Review Release Notes and Documentation

- **Why**: Release notes and official documentation from Microsoft provide comprehensive details on what has changed, what's been fixed, and what's new in Copilot updates.

- **How**:

  - Regularly check the release notes on the Microsoft 365 support site to learn about changes to Copilot and other Microsoft tools.

  - Refer to the official Microsoft documentation to better understand how updates impact your current workflows.

- **Tip**: Bookmark the Microsoft Copilot documentation page for quick access to troubleshooting tips, feature guides, and API updates.

5. Join Microsoft Copilot User Communities

- **Why**: Engaging with the Copilot user community can provide valuable insights from other users who are also learning and adapting to new features.

- **How**:

  - Join forums and user groups such as the Microsoft Tech Community, where Copilot users share tips, ask questions, and discuss new features.

  - Participate in specialized groups on social media platforms like LinkedIn or Reddit to stay updated on best practices and real-world Copilot use cases.

- **Tip**: Participate in user polls, surveys, or feedback opportunities offered by Microsoft to provide insights into how Copilot could be improved.

6. Utilize Copilot's Adaptive Learning

- **Why**: Copilot learns from your interactions, continuously adapting to your preferences and usage patterns, making its suggestions more relevant over time.

- **How**:

  - Give feedback on Copilot's suggestions, such as accepting, modifying, or rejecting its recommendations. This helps it adapt to your needs.

  - If Copilot suggests automation or task completion features, take note of what it does and how you can fine-tune it for better accuracy.

- **Tip**: Use Copilot in a variety of contexts (e.g., drafting emails, creating presentations, analyzing data) to help it better understand your preferences and improve its recommendations.

7. Test New Features in a Controlled Environment

- **Why**: Before fully integrating new features into your workflow, it's a good idea to test them in a sandbox or controlled environment to avoid disrupting your ongoing tasks.

- **How**:

  - Create test documents, spreadsheets, or presentations to experiment with newly introduced features in Microsoft Copilot.

  - Run small test projects using Copilot's latest tools to see how they impact your work.

- **Tip**: If you're part of an organization, consider setting up a test group or pilot program to evaluate new Copilot features before a company-wide rollout.

8. Engage with Copilot's Customization Options

- **Why**: Copilot allows for customization based on your specific needs and preferences, so ongoing learning about how to adjust its behavior can optimize its effectiveness.

- **How**:

  - Regularly review the customization options within the Copilot settings to adjust how it interacts with you. You can tweak its suggestions, responses, and notifications based on your preferences.

  - Experiment with setting up Copilot's language, tone, and task automation to match your workflow.

- **Tip**: Set a periodic reminder to review Copilot's settings every few months to ensure its functionality remains aligned with your evolving needs.

9. Stay Engaged with Third-Party Integrations

- **Why**: Microsoft Copilot integrates with a variety of third-party applications and tools that can extend its functionality, so learning how to integrate and use these features can greatly enhance your experience.

- **How**:

  - Explore the available third-party applications that integrate with Microsoft 365 and Copilot. Whether it's CRM systems, project management tools, or data analytics platforms, these integrations help streamline tasks.

  - Stay informed about new integrations and how they can help you better achieve your goals. Microsoft regularly updates its list of compatible third-party applications.

- **Tip**: Explore Copilot's integration options for automation and enhanced workflows in applications like Salesforce, Trello, and Zoom, depending on your business needs.

10. Monitor and Track Copilot's Performance

- **Why**: To ensure Copilot continues to be effective in helping you complete tasks, it's important to monitor how well it performs over time.

- **How**:

  - Track the time saved and tasks automated by Copilot and compare it with the previous productivity benchmarks.

  - If you notice a decrease in effectiveness, review the settings and customize them to align with any new features or updates.

- **Tip**: Set up periodic reviews to assess Copilot's impact on your workflow and adjust its integration as needed.

Continuous learning and staying updated on Microsoft Copilot's features and best practices are essential to fully benefiting from its powerful capabilities. By keeping up with new releases, engaging with training resources, participating in user communities, and customizing Copilot to fit your workflow, you can ensure that you're making the most of this AI-powered assistant.

CHAPTER NINE
FUTURE OF MICROSOFT COPILOT

Upcoming Features and Enhancements

Microsoft Copilot is continuously evolving to enhance productivity and user experience across various applications. Here are some anticipated features and enhancements for the future of Microsoft Copilot:

1. Expanded Application Integration

- **Broader App Support:** Integration with more Microsoft 365 apps and third-party applications to streamline workflows.

- **Cross-Platform Functionality:** Enhanced capabilities for working seamlessly across devices, including mobile and web.

2. Improved Natural Language Processing

- **Advanced Understanding:** Better context understanding for complex queries and instructions.

- **Conversational AI:** More interactive and fluid conversations, allowing for multi-turn dialogue.

3. Personalization Features

- **User Preferences:** Customizable settings based on user behavior and preferences.

- **Contextual Awareness:** Tailored suggestions based on individual work habits and project requirements.

4. Enhanced Collaboration Tools

- **Real-Time Collaboration:** Improved features for team collaboration, including shared documents and simultaneous editing.

- **Meeting Summaries:** Automatic generation of meeting notes and task assignments.

5. Data Analysis and Visualization

- **Automated Insights:** Advanced data analysis capabilities to provide actionable insights and recommendations.

- **Visual Data Representation:** Enhanced tools for creating charts and graphs directly from data inputs.

6. Learning and Development Tools

- **Skill Enhancement:** Integration of learning modules to help users develop skills relevant to their tasks.

- **Onboarding Assistance:** Tailored resources for new users to get familiar with applications quickly.

7. Security and Compliance Enhancements

- **Data Protection:** Improved security features to protect sensitive information.

- **Compliance Tracking:** Tools to help organizations stay compliant with regulations and standards.

8. Integration with AI Services

- **Third-Party AI Integration:** Ability to leverage external AI services for specialized tasks.

- **Custom AI Models:** Options for organizations to implement and use proprietary AI models.

Microsoft Copilot's future looks promising, with a focus on enhancing productivity, personalization, and collaboration while ensuring security and compliance. As AI technologies continue to advance, we can expect Copilot to become an even more integral part of the Microsoft ecosystem.

Roadmap and Vision

Microsoft Copilot is designed to enhance productivity and streamline workflows across various applications. Here's an overview of its roadmap and vision:

Vision

- **Empowering Users:** The primary goal is to empower users by providing intelligent assistance that enhances creativity and efficiency.

- **Seamless Integration:** A vision of a unified ecosystem where AI assists users across all Microsoft 365 applications and services.

- **User-Centric Design:** Focus on creating a personalized experience that adapts to individual work styles and preferences.

Roadmap

1. **Short-Term Goals (Next 6-12 Months)**

   - **Expanded App Integration:** Launching Copilot features in additional Microsoft applications (e.g., Teams, OneNote).

   - **Enhanced NLP Capabilities:** Improving natural language processing to understand more complex queries and context.

   - **User Feedback Loop:** Implementing mechanisms to collect user feedback to refine features continuously.

2. **Mid-Term Goals (1-2 Years)**

   - **Collaboration Features:** Developing advanced tools for real-time collaboration, including shared workspaces and joint task management.

   - **Data Insight Tools:** Introducing automated data analysis tools that provide actionable insights and visualizations.

   - **Personalization Options:** Allowing deeper customization based on user roles and preferences.

3. **Long-Term Goals (2+ Years)**

    o **AI Ecosystem:** Creating a robust ecosystem where Copilot integrates with third-party AI services, allowing for specialized functionalities.

    o **Learning and Development Integration:** Building features that facilitate skill development and onboarding for new users through interactive tutorials and resources.

    o **Security Enhancements:** Continuous improvements in security protocols to protect sensitive data and ensure compliance.

The roadmap for Microsoft Copilot emphasizes a strategic approach to enhancing user productivity through innovative features and seamless integration. By prioritizing user needs and leveraging advanced AI capabilities, Microsoft aims to create a powerful assistant that transforms how users interact with technology.

Industry Impact and Trends

As Microsoft Copilot continues to evolve, its influence on various industries is expected to grow significantly. Here are some key impacts and trends anticipated for 2025:

1. Increased Automation in Workflows

- **Task Automation:** Copilot will automate routine tasks, freeing up time for employees to focus on more strategic work, enhancing overall productivity.

- **End-to-End Process Automation:** Integration of Copilot into business processes will enable seamless workflow automation across departments.

2. Enhanced Collaboration Across Teams

- **Remote Work Facilitation:** With the rise of remote work, Copilot will foster better collaboration tools, allowing teams to work together more effectively regardless of location.

- **Real-Time Feedback:** Increased capabilities for providing real-time feedback and suggestions during collaborative projects.

3. Data-Driven Decision Making

- **Advanced Analytics:** Copilot will provide deeper insights from data, helping organizations make informed decisions quickly.

- **Predictive Analytics:** Use of AI to forecast trends and outcomes, allowing businesses to proactively adapt strategies.

4. Personalization of User Experience

- **Tailored Recommendations:** Copilot will offer personalized suggestions based on user behavior and preferences, improving engagement and efficiency.

- **Adaptive Learning:** AI-driven learning paths that adapt to individual user needs and skill levels.

5. Security and Compliance Focus

- **Enhanced Security Protocols:** As data privacy concerns grow, Copilot will incorporate advanced security features to protect sensitive information.

- **Compliance Monitoring:** Tools to help organizations ensure compliance with industry regulations will become essential.

6. Integration with Emerging Technologies

- **AI and Machine Learning:** Continuous integration of cutting-edge AI technologies will enhance Copilot's capabilities and applications.

- **Cross-Platform Functionality:** Ability to work seamlessly across various platforms and devices, including IoT and mobile applications.

7. Impact on Job Roles and Skills

- **Skill Shifts:** As automation takes over routine tasks, there will be a shift in required skills, emphasizing critical thinking and creative problem-solving.

- **Reskilling and Upskilling:** Organizations will need to invest in training employees to leverage Copilot effectively and adapt to new tools.

By 2025, Microsoft Copilot is expected to significantly reshape how industries operate, driving efficiency, collaboration, and data-driven decision-making. As organizations adapt to these changes, the emphasis on personalization, security, and integration with emerging technologies will be critical for success.

CHAPTER TEN
APPENDICES

Glossary of Terms

Here's a glossary of key terms and concepts related to Microsoft Copilot to help you better understand its functionalities and features:

1. AI (Artificial Intelligence)

- **Definition**: A branch of computer science that deals with the creation of intelligent machines capable of performing tasks that normally require human intelligence. In the context of Microsoft Copilot, AI is used to assist with tasks like content generation, data analysis, and automating repetitive processes.

2. Automation

- **Definition**: The use of technology to perform tasks without human intervention. In Microsoft Copilot, automation refers to the ability to automatically complete repetitive tasks such as data entry, report generation, or email drafting.

3. Azure AI

- **Definition**: Microsoft's cloud-based AI platform, which powers many of the AI features in Microsoft Copilot. Azure AI includes machine learning tools, cognitive services, and other AI technologies that enhance Copilot's capabilities.

4. Copilot Suggestions

- **Definition**: Recommendations or actions provided by Microsoft Copilot based on user data, usage patterns, and task context. These suggestions can include drafting text, summarizing content, or offering data analysis insights.

5. Natural Language Processing (NLP)

- **Definition**: A field of AI that focuses on enabling machines to understand, interpret, and generate human language. Copilot uses NLP to understand user queries and provide contextually relevant responses, like drafting emails or creating content.

6. Integration

- **Definition**: The process of connecting Microsoft Copilot with other applications, services, or data sources to enhance its functionality. Integrations can be with third-party applications (e.g., Salesforce, Trello) or within Microsoft 365 apps.

7. API (Application Programming Interface)

- **Definition**: A set of protocols and tools that allow different software applications to communicate with each other. Microsoft Copilot's API enables developers to integrate its features into custom applications or workflows.

8. User Interface (UI)

- **Definition**: The means by which a user interacts with Microsoft Copilot and other applications. In Microsoft Copilot, the UI includes the interface elements where suggestions, notifications, and AI-driven features are presented.

9. Cloud Computing

- **Definition**: The delivery of computing services (such as storage, processing, and software) over the internet rather than via local servers. Microsoft Copilot leverages cloud computing for data processing and integration across Microsoft 365 apps.

10. Microsoft 365

- **Definition**: A subscription service that includes Microsoft Office applications (Word, Excel, PowerPoint, Outlook, etc.) along with cloud services like OneDrive and Teams. Microsoft Copilot is integrated into Microsoft 365 to assist users in tasks across these apps.

11. Machine Learning (ML)

- **Definition**: A subset of AI that allows systems to learn and improve from experience without being explicitly programmed. Copilot uses machine learning to continuously adapt its suggestions based on user behavior and data.

12. Task Automation

- **Definition**: The process of using technology to perform repetitive or rule-based tasks without manual intervention. In Copilot, task automation might include drafting a response to an email, creating reports, or analyzing data.

13. Real-Time Assistance

- **Definition**: Copilot's ability to provide help, suggestions, or automated responses in real-time while the user works on a task, whether it's drafting content, analyzing data, or scheduling meetings.

14. Contextual Intelligence

- **Definition**: The ability of Copilot to understand the context of a task or document, such as recognizing what information is relevant for a particular project or email. Copilot uses contextual intelligence to provide more accurate suggestions.

15. Data Insights

- **Definition**: Information or patterns extracted from data, often used to guide decision-making. Copilot can analyze data within apps like Excel to provide insights on trends, outliers, or correlations.

16. Collaborative Features

- **Definition**: Tools within Microsoft Copilot that enable multiple users to work together seamlessly, such as co-authoring documents in Word, collaborating on spreadsheets in Excel, or chatting within Teams.

17. Permissions Management

- **Definition**: The process of controlling access to features, data, and resources within Microsoft Copilot. Administrators can define who can access Copilot's features and control what actions they can take.

18. User Feedback Loop

- **Definition**: A system where Copilot learns and improves based on user interactions and feedback. By providing feedback on suggestions or actions, users can help refine Copilot's behavior and improve its accuracy.

19. Task Delegation

- **Definition**: The process of assigning specific tasks or actions to Copilot, such as asking it to draft an email, summarize data, or automate a report. Copilot helps delegate tasks that would otherwise require manual intervention.

20. Third-Party Applications

- **Definition**: Software developed by external companies that can be integrated with Microsoft 365 and Copilot to expand its functionality. Examples include tools for CRM, project management, and customer support.

21. Security and Compliance

- **Definition**: The set of policies, technologies, and practices that ensure Microsoft Copilot operates securely and complies with data protection laws (such as GDPR). Security features include data encryption and access controls.

22. Copilot API (Application Programming Interface)

- **Definition**: A set of tools and protocols for developers to integrate Microsoft Copilot's functionality into other applications. The Copilot API allows for customization and advanced usage in enterprise environments.

23. Workflows

- **Definition**: The sequence of tasks and processes that a user or organization follows to complete a project or objective. Microsoft Copilot automates parts of workflows, streamlining operations and increasing efficiency.

24. Insights and Analytics

- **Definition**: The ability of Copilot to analyze data and provide actionable insights. Copilot can suggest trends, highlight anomalies, and offer recommendations to improve decision-making.

25. Microsoft Teams

- **Definition**: A collaboration platform that integrates with Microsoft 365, allowing users to chat, meet, share files, and work together in real-time. Copilot integrates with Teams to offer suggestions, automate tasks, and help with team collaboration.

26. Data Privacy

- **Definition**: The protection of user data and the control over who can access it. Copilot adheres to privacy standards to ensure that personal and organizational data is kept safe and only used for legitimate purposes.

This glossary provides essential terms to better understand the features and capabilities of Microsoft Copilot. It's useful for both new and experienced users to familiarize themselves with the terminology to optimize their use of Copilot.

Frequently Asked Questions (FAQs)

Here are some common questions and answers to help you better understand Microsoft Copilot and its capabilities.

1. What is Microsoft Copilot?

Answer: Microsoft Copilot is an AI-powered assistant integrated into Microsoft 365 applications (such as Word, Excel, PowerPoint, Outlook, and Teams). It helps users by providing real-time suggestions, automating tasks, generating content, analyzing data, and offering insights to improve productivity.

2. How do I access Microsoft Copilot?

Answer: Microsoft Copilot is available to Microsoft 365 subscribers with the appropriate license. To access Copilot, ensure that you are using a supported version of Microsoft 365 and have Copilot enabled for your account by the administrator

3. What applications does Microsoft Copilot work with?

Answer: Microsoft Copilot works with several Microsoft 365 applications, including:

- Microsoft Word
- Microsoft Excel
- Microsoft PowerPoint
- Microsoft Outlook
- Microsoft Teams

4. How does Microsoft Copilot help me with daily tasks?

Answer: Copilot assists by automating repetitive tasks, offering suggestions based on your work context, drafting emails or documents, generating reports, summarizing data, and even helping you create presentations. It saves time and helps you focus on more strategic work.

5. Is Microsoft Copilot available for all Microsoft 365 users?

Answer: No, Microsoft Copilot is available to users with specific Microsoft 365 business or enterprise licenses. It is part of premium plans, so it may not be accessible on lower-tier plans like Microsoft 365 Personal or Family.

6. Can I customize the suggestions provided by Microsoft Copilot?

Answer: Yes, you can customize how Copilot interacts with you. For example, you can adjust the tone of its suggestions, choose how often you want notifications, and provide feedback on its recommendations to improve its relevance over time.

7. How secure is Microsoft Copilot?

Answer: Microsoft Copilot adheres to stringent security and compliance standards. It uses encryption to protect your data and complies with privacy regulations like GDPR. Admins can control user permissions to ensure data access is restricted and secure.

8. Can Microsoft Copilot help with data analysis in Excel?

Answer: Yes, Microsoft Copilot can analyze large datasets in Excel, identify trends, generate charts, and provide insights based on your data. It can suggest formulas, automate data entry, and help you perform complex analysis with minimal effort.

9. How does Copilot's AI learn and adapt?

Answer: Copilot uses machine learning to analyze your interactions, work patterns, and preferences. Over time, it becomes better at understanding your tasks and providing more accurate and relevant suggestions. It also adapts to the specific context of your work.

10. What happens if I don't want to use Copilot's suggestions?

Answer: You can ignore or dismiss Copilot's suggestions. Additionally, you can turn off specific features or modify its settings to prevent certain types of suggestions. Copilot is designed to be flexible and can adapt to your preferred workflow.

11. Can I use Microsoft Copilot in a team environment?

Answer: Yes, Microsoft Copilot supports collaborative environments. In Microsoft Teams, for example, Copilot can assist by drafting team communications, scheduling meetings, summarizing discussions, and providing real-time suggestions during collaborative work.

12. Does Microsoft Copilot integrate with third-party apps?

Answer: Yes, Microsoft Copilot can integrate with various third-party applications to enhance your workflow. These integrations allow Copilot to interact with CRM systems, project management tools, and other productivity platforms, making it easier to streamline tasks and data across systems.

13. How can I provide feedback to improve Copilot?

Answer: You can provide feedback directly through the application by using the "Feedback" button, which is typically found in the settings or help menu. Microsoft also periodically collects user feedback to improve Copilot's functionality

14. Is there any additional cost for Microsoft Copilot?

Answer: Yes, Microsoft Copilot is available as part of certain Microsoft 365 business and enterprise subscriptions. It may not be included in lower-tier subscriptions like Microsoft 365 Personal or Family. The cost depends on the subscription plan you choose.

15. Can Microsoft Copilot create presentations in PowerPoint?

Answer: Yes, Copilot can help you create presentations by generating slides, offering content suggestions, creating outlines, and even providing design layouts. It can quickly generate professional-quality presentations based on your input or data.

16. How do I keep Microsoft Copilot up to date?

Answer: Microsoft Copilot updates automatically as part of your Microsoft 365 subscription. Ensure that you have automatic updates enabled for your Microsoft 365 apps, so Copilot stays current with the latest features and improvements.

17. How do I troubleshoot issues with Microsoft Copilot?

Answer: If you're experiencing issues with Copilot, you can troubleshoot by:

- Checking for updates to ensure you're using the latest version.
- Reviewing your settings to ensure Copilot is enabled.
- Using the "Help" or "Support" section within the app for assistance.
- Visiting the Microsoft support website for known issues and solutions

18. Can Copilot help me write emails in Outlook?

Answer: Yes, Copilot can draft and suggest responses to emails in Outlook. It can generate email text based on context, summarize long email threads, and help organize your inbox by suggesting automatic replies.

19. What types of tasks can Copilot automate?

Answer: Copilot can automate a wide range of tasks, including:

- Scheduling and organizing meetings in Outlook and Teams.
- Drafting, editing, and formatting documents in Word.
- Data entry, analysis, and reporting in Excel.
- Creating and designing presentations in PowerPoint.

20. Can Microsoft Copilot assist with content creation for social media?

Answer: While Copilot is primarily designed for use within Microsoft 365 apps, its AI capabilities can assist with drafting social media posts, generating content ideas, and providing writing suggestions. You can use Copilot to create content in Word, then adapt it for social media platforms.

These FAQs cover many of the common inquiries about Microsoft Copilot's features and functionality. If you have additional questions, the Microsoft support team and user communities are valuable resources for further assistance.

THANK YOU FOR READING